# The Planning Companion®

## R.N. Garnitz

## A Life and Retirement Planning Guide
FEDERAL EDITION

LifeSpan Services, Inc.
Decatur, Georgia

- *Getting Started on the Right Foot*
- *The Planning Companion®*
- *The Mid-Career Planner*
- *The Basic Principles: LifeSpan Financial Planning*
- *The Law Enforcement Planner*

Cover: Jamaine Sales

ISBN 0-927289-76-8
Printed in the United States of America

**LifeSpan Services, Inc.**
235 East Ponce de Leon Avenue
Decatur, Georgia 30030
404-373-2548


lifespan-services.com
lifespan@lifespan-services.com

# CONTENTS

Abraham Lincoln said, "You can't escape the responsibility of tomorrow by evading it today." This book is your guide to taking responsibility for building the kind of future you've always envisioned. Retirement planning is life planning . . . involving far more than just having adequate income. How will you deal with an aging parent, or a boomerang child returning home as an adult?

Perhaps you're interested in a second career or plan on moving to a warmer climate. All these issues warrant careful planning. The Planning Companion can help. It's timely in content, comprehensive in scope, and easy to understand.

The next third of your life should be the best time of your life. Continue to learn, to play and enjoy your leisure, and continue to do meaningful things in the workforce and out of it. That's the key to a successful future. All the best for the years ahead!

*Rick Garnitz*

# CHAPTER 1

# Are You Ready?

*Do I need a financial planner, or can I do this myself?*
*What percent of my current income will I need in retirement?*
*Will my retirement outlast my money?*
*How do I get started?*

R ETIREMENT IS A VERY DIFFERENT JOURNEY. A journey that could well last for 30 or 40 years. As with any journey, you need to know where you are going and how to get there. Creating a retirement road map is a good start.

So much has changed. The economic uncertainties of the first four years of this decade have caused many of us to postpone retirement or consider part-time retirement careers. We'll live longer, and in all likelihood, stay more active than our parents' generation, maintaining reasonably good health into our 80s and even 90s. That requires planning.

One important aspect of your planning will be how to finance your journey. Not an easy task when the economy is as turbulent as it's been the last few years. You need a plan that includes understanding your assets and income, liabilities and expenses now and in anticipation of your future needs. Chances are that the value of your assets, which grew so quickly in the 1990s, fell somewhat in the first years of this decade. Financial planning is not an investment, a hot stock, or a group of high-tech mutual funds. Financial planning is a process. It is a way of looking at your life today and your hopes for tomorrow and deciding what needs to be put in place for both.

Your journey requires thoughtful planning and both hands on the wheel. After all, you're crafting the next third of your life. Doing it right means knowing what you want the future to look like and figuring out what the best strategies are to make that vision a reality. It's a continuous process, one that will be modified as your needs and circumstances change. It's exciting, challenging, and important. Let's get started!

## Your Financial Fitness

Planning is important not only to assure that your financial future is secure, but also to keep family and friends aware of your expectations. Everyone knows someone who died or divorced, and left behind a partner who had little or no knowledge of assets, liabilities, and future plans. Planning for a family cannot be done in a vacuum. Both partners should share information. You should also give serious thought to keeping those who play a role in making sure that your decisions are implemented fully informed.

If you are single, widowed, or divorced, you alone are responsible for the financial directions you pursue! Carefully assessing your current financial condition prepares you not only for planning your future but also for handling any future changes, whether personal or financial.

The following questions will help you, or you and your partner, understand your financial management strengths and weaknesses. Select the most accurate answer. After answering all questions, review each and indicate your satisfaction or dissatisfaction with your responses. If you are satisfied, enter a "+."

| Financial Management | Always | Usually | Sometimes | Never |
|---|---|---|---|---|
| Do you have a good credit record? | ☐ | ☐ | ☐ | ☐ |
| Do you follow a budget? | ☐ | ☐ | ☐ | ☐ |
| Do you keep accurate financial records? | ☐ | ☐ | ☐ | ☐ |
| Do you review your financial position every year? | ☐ | ☐ | ☐ | ☐ |
| Do you make time to arrange your financial affairs? | ☐ | ☐ | ☐ | ☐ |

| Talking Money | Always | Usually | Sometimes | Never |
|---|---|---|---|---|
| Do you agree with each other in money matters? | ☐ | ☐ | ☐ | ☐ |
| If one of you died, would the other be able to maintain your lifestyle? | ☐ | ☐ | ☐ | ☐ |
| Have you reached a clear understanding on your short- and long-term financial goals? | ☐ | ☐ | ☐ | ☐ |
| Do you know your financial flash-points and respect one another's views? | ☐ | ☐ | ☐ | ☐ |
| Can you account for how you spend your money? | ☐ | ☐ | ☐ | ☐ |

**Investing**

| | Always | Usually | Sometimes | Never |
|---|---|---|---|---|
| Do you feel confident with your knowledge of various types of investments? | ☐ | ☐ | ☐ | ☐ |
| Are you comfortable with the allocation in your retirement plan? | ☐ | ☐ | ☐ | ☐ |
| Do you feel you are adequately covered with insurance on both yourselves and your property? | ☐ | ☐ | ☐ | ☐ |
| Are you rational (not emotional) in making your financial decisions? | ☐ | ☐ | ☐ | ☐ |
| Has your investment philosophy kept you out of several riskier investments? | ☐ | ☐ | ☐ | |

You should now have a better understanding of your financial fitness, including areas that may require attention. Making changes isn't terribly difficult. Change requires two things—acknowledging that change can lead to better long-term financial planning and acquiring the discipline to alter old patterns.

Next in our sequence of "key" considerations is analyzing your current assets. We've provided you with four columns, although you may not need all four. Some of these items can only be estimated. That's okay! Our objective is to provide just a snapshot, not a full-color portrait, of the majority of your current assets and their current worth.

## Your Current Assets

| | You | Partner | Ownership Single | Joint |
|---|---|---|---|---|
| Current Annual Salary | | | | |
| Commissions | | | | |
| Checking Accounts | | | | |
| | | | | |
| Savings Accounts | | | | |
| Credit Union Accounts | | | | |
| Brokerage Accounts | | | | |
| Certificates of Deposit | | | | |
| Treasuries: (Notes, Bills, Bonds) | | | | |
| Bonds: Corporate & Municipal | | | | |
| Common Stock | | | | |
| | | | | |
| | | | | |
| Money Market Accounts /Funds | | | | |
| Mutual Funds | | | | |
| | | | | |
| Insurance Annuities | | | | |
| | | | | |
| 401k, 403b, 457, etc. | | | | |
| Profit Sharing, etc. | | | | |
| Real Estate Rental Income | | | | |
| Other Income Sources | | | | |
| Home | | | | |
| Other Real Estate | | | | |
| | | | | |
| Personal Property | | | | |
| | | | | |
| | | | | |
| Total Current Assets | | | | |

# Estimating Your Retirement Income

What percentage of your preretirement income will be replaced by all sources of postretirement income? According to the traditional rule of thumb, in order to support your lifestyle after retirement, you'll need from 70 to 80 percent of your former income. Your retirement income is most often derived from three sources: your pension, your Social Security benefits, and your income from investments. A second career or inheritance may add additional income.

Most people underestimate the amount of money they need to accumulate in order to retire with security. Do you know how much you'll need? Changing tax rates, coupled with often dramatically lower interest rates, mean that you will net even less investment income. To combat this, you need to reexamine your investments regularly.

For a quick estimate of how much income you'll have at retirement and how much you'll need for the kind of retirement you have in mind, calculate the following:

1. *Target 75 percent of your current gross income*     $ _____

2. *Expected Social Security benefits*     $ _____

3. *Expected retirement benefits (IRA, Keogh, 401k,*     $ _____
   *employer plans) currently in place*     $ _____

4. *Annual investment income needed*     $ _____
   *(line 1 minus lines 2 and 3).*

If your current savings will provide the needed amount, you're making good decisions in planning for the future. If not, make adjustments now.

Recalculate your savings goals every year to take into account any shifts in your pension, changes in your Social Security benefit, your retirement savings plans, and the performance of your investments.

## Your Assets at Retirement

| | You | Partner | Ownership Single | Joint |
|---|---|---|---|---|
| Estimated Pension and Retirement Annuities | | | | |
| Estimated Social Security Benefit* | | | | |
| Savings and Investments | | | | |
| Savings Accounts | | | | |
| Certificates of Deposit | | | | |
| Bonds | | | | |
| Stocks | | | | |
| IRAs | | | | |
| Mutual Funds | | | | |
| Insurance Annuities | | | | |
| Profit Sharing | | | | |
| (401ks, Thrift Plans, etc.) | | | | |
| Second Career (estimated) | | | | |
| Real Estate (Rental Income) | | | | |
| Inheritance | | | | |
| Other Income Sources | | | | |
| Home | | | | |
| Other Real Estate | | | | |
| Personal Property | | | | |
| Total Projected Retirement Income | | | | |

* Check your annual estimate.

# The Power of Compounding

Toward the end of Albert Einstein's life, a reporter approached him and asked the famous scientist what was the single most amazing thing he had witnessed in his 70-plus years. His response: "The power of compounding." Over time compounded interest can turn even modest savings into substantial funds. You need two ingredients: time and the highest possible interest you can get.

Time is often an easier ingredient to secure than high interest rates, especially if you are young. Investments made early in life and left alone to compound may actually outperform larger investments made later.

To understand how compounding can work for you, use the *Rule of 72*. To see how long it will take for your money to double, divide an interest rate, say 6 percent, into 72 (72 ÷ 6). This example gives a result of 12. At 6 percent your money will double in 12 years through compounding; at 8 percent interest (72 ÷ 8 = 9) your money will double in nine years.

What if you saved a penny on the first day of the month, and every day you doubled what you had saved so far? How much money do you think you would have at the end of one month?

The penny is compounding. On day two you would have two cents, on day three you'd have four cents, then eight cents, etc. On the 30th day of the month you would have more than $5 million ($5,368,709.12)! That is the power of compounding. Understand it and make it work for you.

How much do you need to save to have a secure retirement? As much as you can and as early as you can! Your Social Security and pension benefits combined may not be enough to meet your retirement living costs. You have more responsibility for financing your retirement than workers in earlier generations had. The reality of our changing workplace means that fewer people will retire after careers of 30 years with one organization. Planning now for the likelihood that you will be funding your own retirement is very smart.

With compounding it is possible to build wealth with dividend-paying stocks, bonds, and other income investments. The keys to this wealth-building strategy:

1. Don't consume the interest.
2. Automatically reinvest the interest in an interest-earning account.

## The Economy

The Federal Reserve has focused on controlling inflation in an effort to spur the economy. Inflation (rising prices) has been the principal enemy of America's growth, making it harder for people to increase their standard of living. Purchasing homes, cars and even staples like groceries is tougher as prices increase. Now many economists believe our new economic villain may well be deflation, or falling prices.

As prices fall, for clothing, textiles, electronics, and rents—corporations and the public sector keep raises to a minimum since profits and tax revenue are reduced. Such an economy sends out mixed messages about inflation and deflation. Some prices are rising—health care, education, food—but generally, low inflation has been the order of the day since the early 1990s. Inflation for 2006 should be at or below 3 percent. The unknown factor is the price of fuel, which escalated dramatically in 2006.

A downward spiral on prices shrinks or eliminates profits. Companies cut expenses and that often translates into frozen wages or lost jobs. As your pay-check shrinks not all of your expenses shrink with it. Fixed costs, like mortgages, need to be paid whether or not your paycheck has shrunk or even disappeared. It is a delicate balancing act.

Inflation needs to be a factor in planning for your financial future. The difference in expenses for goods and services can vary widely from year to year. However, even the moderate 1-3 percent inflation rate we've witnessed over the past few years has an impact on both your income and your investments. To combat inflation, consider a broad array of investment and savings options. Be sure that your savings plan earns more than the inflation rate.

Many prices are rising faster than the government's official inflation rate, which shows prices increasing an average of 2.5 percent over the past three years.

## *Rising Prices*

| Consumer Purchases | 2003 | 2004 | 2005 |
|---|---|---|---|
| Single-family home | $ 170,000.00 | $182,500.00 | $215,000.00 |
| Toyota Camry | 19,455.00 | 19,685.00 | 20,665.00 |
| Unleaded Gasoline | 1.58 | 1.87 | 2.25 |
| Pair of Jeans | 39.50 | 39.50 | 39.50 |
| Tax Preparation | 129.84 | 140.24 | 175.00 |
| MacDonald's Big Mac | 2.22 | 2.29 | 2.29 |
| Domestic Airline Ticket | 244.00 | 237.00 | 252.00 |
| Vacation | 1,162.00 | 1,375.00 | 1,490.00 |
| Birth of a Child | 6,696.00 | 7,187.00 | 7,560.00 |
| A Year in College | 15,226.00 | 16.638.00 | 18,100.00 |

# CHAPTER 2

# Risk vs Reward

*How can I take more risks without losing a bundle?*
*When do I sell, versus waiting out a turnaround?*
*What do I need to understand about new investments?*
*How do no-load mutual funds charge for their services?*
*What does a well-balanced portfolio mean?*
*What is an appropriate retirement asset allocation mix?*

DIFFERENT INVESTMENTS MEET DIFFERENT OBJECTIVES. Most people have five objectives when investing their money: safety, growth, yield, liquidity, and tax benefits. No one investment can meet all five objectives. Some safer investments provide a lower yield while high growth investments may carry less safety. The key is to select a combination that will give you the results you seek.

## Investment Philosophy

All investments carry some level of risk. Your investment philosophy reflects your risk tolerance. Are you a risk taker? Or do you prefer safe investments that are backed by the federal government? Risk and reward are factors in any investment. The potential for greater return brings with it greater risk. All of your investments combine to make up your portfolio. Your retirement savings portfolio may include a certificate of deposit in your IRA, equity investments in your 401k or thrift savings plan, and an annuity at an insurance company. Your investment philosophy influences the types of investments you choose.

## Diversification

Diversification is distributing your funds among securities of different industries or classes. It is a method by which you, whether you have a small or large portfolio, can obtain your financial goals. Although there is no right way to invest, most investment professionals recommend diversification. It won't guarantee positive results, but it may help you achieve your goals, by spreading risk and lessening large-scale losses.

## Allocating Assets

Asset allocation is distributing your investments among asset classes. Choosing how your investments are split is a way of investing to fit your stage in life, your goals for the future, and your plans for retirement. The three major asset classes are stocks, bonds, and cash equivalents. Determining the allocation that works for you is critical to your investment success. Investment growth is primarily based on asset allocation and not on specific stock selection or market timing. For most investors, protecting money while building assets means investing in vehicles such as stocks, bonds, and real estate or taking measured risks. Only you can decide how much of your investable cash to put into each type of investment. The decision is based on your goals and risk tolerance.

## What about timing the market?

If only we knew what the future holds. If you could predict the future, you could time the markets. If you could time the markets, at age 85 you would look back on a lifetime of successful financial decisions. According to a 1994 University of Michigan study, 95 percent of the stock market's cumulative gain between 1963 and 1993 occurred in just 1.2 percent of the trading days. That's 90 days out of the 7,500 days contained in those 30 years. If you had tried to time the market, pulling out of stocks during recessions and economic lows, you might have missed some (or many) of those banner days.

How long will a bull or bear market last? We can only guess. It's too risky to put money in—or pull money out—based on guesses. How long should you stay in the market? What about when the market is going down, or is flat for an extended period? One school of thought suggests buying quality investments with successful growth records and holding them for a long time. A buy-and-hold philosophy works better than the churn and burn—trading equities whenever the market is off or up by 10 percent.

The following chart shows the results of various portfolio averages, their best-year and worst-year performances, and their compound return over 49 years. Most people don't hold investments 49 years, but saving for your future, college funding, or a second home requires taking the longer view. Buy and hold.

## 48 Year Portfolio Performances

| Sample Portfolios | 1 | 2 | 3 | 4 | 5 | 6 |
|---|---|---|---|---|---|---|
| Percentage of Stocks | 30% | 40% | 50% | 60% | 70% | 100% |
| Percentage of Bonds | 70% | 60% | 50% | 40% | 30% | 0% |
| **Return** | | | | | | |
| Avg Annual Total Return 1951-1999 | 8.6% | 9.4% | 10.1% | 10.8% | 11.4% | 13.3% |
| Growth of $100,000 | 5.7mil | 8.0 | 11.0 | 15.0 | 20.1 | 44.7 |

Source: Roger G. Ibbotson and Rex A. Sinquefield, "Stocks, Bonds, Bills, and Inflation: Year-by-Year Historical Returns," University of Chicago Press, Journal of Business (January 1976), Compustat, Stat Street Securities and Bernstein estimates.

To understand why buy and hold is recommended, look at time. The longer you hold equities, the less your risk of loss. If your time horizon is one year, your risk of loss is far greater than it is if you hold equities or mutual funds for five or 10 years. Business cycles usually occur in waves of four to seven years. The bull market of the 1990s was the longest on record. In the last several years, both the NASDAQ and the DOW dropped significantly. The market responds to a variety of factors, but the turbulence in stock prices is expected to continue. Normally, if you can stay in the market for five to 10 years, you minimize your losses because you ride out the cycles.

### The Pyramid of Investment

The pyramid of investment is a visual, structured approach to financial planning. A pyramid is built on a safe, solid base. Your financial future must be built on a secure base provided by solid investments. After this base has been established, providing safety and liquidity, more moderate risk investments can be considered. It is often suggested that between 45 and 60 percent of your investment dollars should be in conservative investments as you approach retirement.

The second section, the moderate risk investments, should contain between 35 and 45 percent of your investable income. As you move up the pyramid, investments involve increased risk and the potential for greater gains. The high-risk portion should generally contain no more than 5 percent of your money.

## The Pyramid of Investment

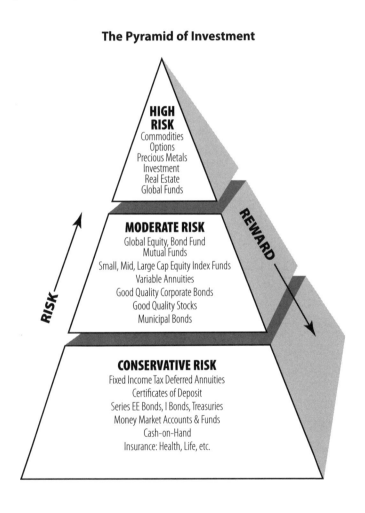

**HIGH RISK**
Commodities
Options
Precious Metals
Investment
Real Estate
Global Funds

**MODERATE RISK**
Global Equity, Bond Fund
Mutual Funds
Small, Mid, Large Cap Equity Index Funds
Variable Annuities
Good Quality Corporate Bonds
Good Quality Stocks
Municipal Bonds

**CONSERVATIVE RISK**
Fixed Income Tax Deferred Annuities
Certificates of Deposit
Series EE Bonds, I Bonds, Treasuries
Money Market Accounts & Funds
Cash-on-Hand
Insurance: Health, Life, etc.

RISK

REWARD

If liquid assets are needed within a short period of time—one to three years—keep your investments more conservative. If you won't need the money for three to seven years, you can afford to take a more moderate approach. If you are more than eight years away from needing your money, consider more aggressive investments that carry greater risk but the possibility of greater returns.

## Conservative Risk Investments

The lower section of the pyramid contains conservative risk investments. As you move up the pyramid, investments carry higher risk. Begin building your pyramid with a solid, well-thought-out foundation. The investments in this section are not slick and will not make money fast. Investments in the base section provide the structure you need before expanding your investment horizon. Most financial planners recommend shifting some of your higher risk investments to more conservative areas as you approach retirement. One definition of loss is having to cash out of an investment at an inopportune time.

### Insurance

Protecting your assets by insuring yourself and your family against catastrophe is fundamental to sound financial planning. Insurance on your life, health, home, and property is the cornerstone of most financial plans. Insurance takes many forms, from pure protection to serving as an investment vehicle. It is a contract between you and a company. You pay a relatively small cost, the premium, for sharing your risk with others facing similar risks. The cost of losses that occur is shared by all policyholders. Insurance products with investment options comprise 40 percent of all life insurance now sold.

Term insurance provides simple death protection for a certain period and nothing more. There is no element of savings, and you cannot borrow against term insurance. Term insurance is usually calculated on a five- or 10-year renewable term with the option of renewing your policy without an additional medical exam. Renewable term often stops at age 55 or 60. Term policies may be convertible or non-convertible. A convertible policy may be exchanged for a higher premium whole life policy without a medical exam.

- Premiums for **level term** insurance increase at the end of every term if the original face value of the policy remains the same. A term is usually five, 10, 15, or 20 years.

- With a **decreasing term policy**, premium payments remain the same, but the face value of the policy decreases.

- Your employer most likely has **group term** coverage for you. Find out if you can continue partial coverage in retirement. It could save you money.

A **Whole Life** policy agrees to pay a stated sum of money to your beneficiaries at your death. The premiums usually remain level and are paid for life, building a cash value you can borrow against.

A small portion of the premium on a **Variable Universal Life** policy buys death benefit protection; the rest is invested and pays a periodically adjusted rate that reflects market rates. Earnings on the investment portion are tax deferred. If you pay enough to cover the death benefit portion, you do not have to stick to a set monthly payment schedule.

A **Universal Life with Investment Choices** is a hybrid policy with a death benefit portion and an investment portion. Unlike variable universal life, you choose where to invest the investment portion. You make scheduled premium payments, and the value of the policy may fluctuate, depending on your investment's performance.

An **Umbrella** policy is inexpensive and provides protection against high-dollar liability claims, adding at least one million dollars to your personal auto policy, homeowners liability policy, and sometimes boat or recreational vehicle policy. The policy picks up liability claims not covered by your underlying policy.

### Insurance Company Ratings

Five companies grade insurers, but each uses different criteria. When you are shopping for insurance, choose a company rated secure by at least three of the five companies.

| Company | Ratings | | |
|---|---|---|---|
| | **secure** | **vulnerable** | **poor** |
| A.M. Best (ambest.com) | A++ to B+ | B to C- | D to F |
| Fitch Ratings (fitchratings.com) | AAA to BBB- | BB+ to C | DDD to D |
| Moody's Investors Services (moodys.com) | Aaa to Baa3 | Ba1 to B3 | Caa1 to C |
| Standard & Poor's (standardandpoors.com) | AAA to BBB- | BB+ to CCC- | CC to R |
| Weiss Ratings (weissratings.com) | A+ to C- | D+ to D- | E+ to F |

## Emergency Funds and Cash on Hand

Everyone should have three to six months of salary in safe, easily accessible (liquid) investments. The reasons are obvious. If you lose your job, a spouse needs surgery, or a child needs financial assistance—and they will—these funds will be available.

Where should you keep these funds? In the past people kept their money in passbook savings accounts. Most bank passbook accounts now pay only $^3/_4$ to $1^1/_2$ percent interest. Credit unions will, in all probability pay a half to a full percent higher. Money market accounts will typically provide an even higher rate of return. All are safe and liquid sources for an emergency fund.

Banks, brokerage firms, and mutual funds all offer money market accounts with no interest rate ceiling. The interest rate floats, changing daily, driven by economic events and broad markets. You can write checks against your available funds, making them very liquid as long as a minimum balance is maintained.

The differences in the bank money markets and those available from mutual funds or brokerage houses means you should shop for the highest interest rates. Typically, banks will pay a lower interest rate than mutual funds or brokerage houses. Different institutions offer different rates. Investigate your alternatives.

## Series EE Bonds

If you want total safety, invest in America as your parents did. Buy EE Bonds (U.S. Savings Bonds), which are sold in minimums of $50 each.

**Savings Bonds** issued after May 1, 1997, earn 90 percent of the average five-year Treasury yield for the preceding six months. Interest is credited monthly rather than every six months. Interest earned on Series EE bonds may be tax exempt if used to pay college tuition and fees in the same year you redeem the bonds.

## Inflation-Protected Securities

The **I Bond** is a U.S. Savings Bond with the features of Series EE Bonds—affordable, safe, liquid, with tax advantages and growth. Interest is compounded semiannually. I Bonds, however, have inflation-indexed earnings. The earnings rate is a combination of a fixed rate and a semiannual inflation rate. Both rates are determined each May 1 and November 1. I Bonds are attractive because they guarantee that inflation doesn't erode your savings. Issued at 50 percent of face value, a $100 Series EE Bond costs $50. Issued at 100 percent of face value, a $100 I Bond costs $100.

Although EE Bonds are guaranteed to reach face value in 17 years, there is no guaranteed level of earnings for I Bonds. There is a three-month earnings penalty for redeeming an I Bond within the first five years. I Bonds are meant to be long-term investments.

## TIPS

Treasury Inflation-Protected Securities (TIPS) are the safest of the safe. TIPS pay interest every six months and a payment of principal when the security matures. The principal value of a TIPS is adjusted based on the Consumer Price Index. At maturity the security is redeemed at its inflation-adjusted principal amount or its original par value, whichever is greater.

TIPS pay a fixed rate of interest, which is applied to the inflation-adjusted principal. In times of inflation each interest payment will be greater than the previous one. In the event of deflation, your interest payment will decrease.

Learn more about TIPS on *TreasuryDirect (www.publicdebt.treas.gov)*.

## Treasuries

**Treasury bills**, also called T-bills, help finance government obligations and are issued in maturities of 13, 26, and 52 weeks. A minimum of

$10,000 is required to purchase T-bills, and they may be purchased in multiples of $5,000 after that. You buy them on a discount basis, receiving the face value at maturity. T-bills can be purchased from brokerage firms, banks, savings and loans, or directly from the government through the Federal Reserve banks. The Treasury auctions three- and six-month bills weekly, and one-year bills monthly. The interest is exempt from state and local taxation.

**Treasury notes** are longer term investments than T-bills, with maturities of two to nine years, depending on your choice and minimum investment. Treasury notes purchased with maturities of less than five years require a $5,000 minimum investment. Notes purchased with maturities of five years and above require a $1,000 minimum investment. The Treasury auctions two-year and five-year notes on the last business day of every month. Three-year and 10-year notes are auctioned quarterly. Interest is paid every six months. At maturity your Treasury note must be redeemed by mail.

**Treasury bonds** have the longest maturity of all Treasury investments. In late 2005 the treasury decided to reintroduce the 30-year treasury bond. This means mortgage rates and other loans will now be correlated to 30-year treasuries. A $1,000 minimum purchase is required. Interest is paid semiannually. You can buy Treasury bonds at auction (August and February) directly from the government or a broker. Your local Federal Reserve Bank can open a Treasury direct account. Treasury securities are booked electronically. There are no printed certificates.

You can buy **inflation-protection bonds**, also called 10-year notes, for $1,000 and up. The principal goes up or down with inflation according to the monthly consumer price index while the interest rate holds steady. Interest is paid twice yearly. You are taxed yearly on gains in the principal, so these notes are better for tax-deferred accounts.

The U.S. Treasury Department's recent move to kill the 30-year bond for the immediate future was designed to cut the government's borrowing costs and to acknowledge that long-term securities aren't needed. The other equally important outcome is to reduce borrowing costs for consumers and businesses. The yield on other shorter-term treasuries has dropped. Fixed-rate mortgages are most often tied to the yield on the 10-year Treasury bond.

## *How Bonds React to Events*

| | |
|---|---|
| **Inflation rises** | price falls, yield rises, duration falls |
| **The bond ages** | price moves toward par, yield moves toward shorter term rates, duration falls |
| **Bond is downgraded** | the price usually falls, the yield usually rises, duration usually falls |
| **Call becomes likely** | price usually moves toward the call price, yield moves toward shorter term rates, duration falls |
| **Principal payment** | price falls, yield rises, duration rises slightly |
| **Prepayment rate rise** | price moves toward par, yield moves toward shorter term rates, duration falls |

Source: Lehman Brothers, Inc.


## Certificates of Deposit (CD)

The CD was designed with safety of principal as its chief priority, and yield secondary. CDs can be purchased from banks and brokerage houses. Almost all CDs now have varying maturities and interest rates. The interest rates are determined by the individual bank or savings and loan.

## Tax-Deferred Annuities

Deferred annuities are contracts issued by insurance companies, that have nothing to do with insurance. The rates are guaranteed by law, and the funds are put into a legal trust fund. The periods for annuities vary. The shortest is for five years. Most have a penalty for early withdrawal. There is no commission, interest rates are usually higher than short-term government securities, and the interest rate on many is annually adjusted. If interest rates fall, most annuities have a limit on how much they may drop in a year. Deferred annuities are not subject to contribution limitations.

When stocks tank, interest rates are low, and financial planners are scrambling for business, annuities become more popular. This was certainly the case in the first three-and-a-half years of this decade. With markets falling and few places to take shelter, annuities were sold as a relatively safe haven in stormy economic times. Besides that, annuities usually pay the seller a hefty commission.

Annuities may, however, fit into some portfolios. Most annuities are tax deferred and, generally, there is no limit on the amount you can contribute. That's good, but unlike an IRA, a 401k, or the Thrift Savings Plan for federal employees, you don't get any tax deduction for your contributions. That's bad. Thus, tax-deferred annuities present a good news/bad news story. They do grow tax deferred but there is no tax savings appearing annually on your W-2.

Currently, annuity income is fully taxed when you begin making withdrawals. This may change as tax policy and dividend interest are reviewed by Congress. Typically, you select when you want payments to begin. Like an IRA, you can begin payments as early as 59½ or you may delay them to later. Your next decision is how you want your annuities dispersed. You can select a variety of options and survivorship rights are probably your most important consideration.

Annuities are marketed in two broad categories—fixed and variable. A **fixed annuity** pays a fixed interest rate for a set period. Be careful. Some annuity vendors will offer "teaser rates" for a year or two. When CDs are paying 3.5 percent, a teaser rate of 7 percent can look good, until you realize it is only for one year and you still have to factor in commissions and loads. After the teaser rate ends, many annuities will have an interest rate floor of 2 or 3 percent. Many insurance companies that underwrite and market annuities have begun removing the guaranteed minimum interest rate on new annuity business.

**Variable annuities** place more responsibility for annuities' performance in your hands. You select the stock, bond, or money market funds you want. If they are poor performers, so is your annuity. If you get fed up and decide you want to cancel your annuity, there are often surrender charges.

The best part of an annuity may be the guarantee of payments to you at a designated time. They can be a dicier proposition when fees and commissions are high. Interest rates on fixed annuities are low, the performance of variable annuities may be poor. Give a lot of thought to why you are considering an annuity and then shop around for low-load or no-load annuity products.

## Moderate-Risk Investments

The mid-section of the pyramid is popular with most investors. These are the investments that you hear about on the evening news. There are no hard-and-fast rules about how much of your investment dollars should be in moderate risk investments. Normally, once you have a firm foundation of savings, insurance, and lower risk investments, you may place between 35 and 45 percent of your assets in the moderate-risk area. How much you allocate is a mix that depends on your risk tolerance, your investment time horizon, and the return you want over the long haul.

## Tax-Deferred Savings Plans

Congress has liberalized individual retirement account (IRA) regulations, increasing the annual contribution rate limits and providing a catch-up provision for workers over 50 who haven't saved as much for retirement. These changes affect both regular and Roth IRAs.

## Individual Retirement Accounts

IRAs are found in both the conservative and moderate risk sections of the pyramid. An IRA is a container that can hold a wide variety of investments such as CDs, individual stocks, or mutual funds. The container keeps the investments tax deferred until you access them, as early as 59½ or as late as 70½.

### IRA Contribution Limits

| Tax Year | Maximum Contribution |
|---|---|
| 2005 through 2007 | $4,000 |
| 2008 and thereafter | $5,000 |

After 2008 the contribution limit will be adjusted annually for inflation in $500 increments. If your income is above the lower figure in the phase-out range, you begin to lose the tax deductibility of your contribution. When your modified adjusted gross income is above the higher amount, you lose all tax deductibility. The phase-out range increases each year for single taxpayers and couples filing joint returns. An Internet search will give you examples of how to calculate the precise percentage of the deductibility for which you qualify.

In 2006, if you're single and your income is less than $50,000, or if you are married with a joint income of less than $75,000, you can in all likelihood contribute to an IRA. The *Economic Growth and Tax Relief Reconciliation Act of 2001* increased the annual contribution limits to qualified retirement plans.

If your income is above the lower figure in the phase-out range, you begin to lose the tax deductibility of your contribution. When your modified adjusted gross income is above the higher amount, you lose all tax deductibility. The phase-out range increases each year for both single taxpayers and couples filing joint returns. A search of the Internet will provide examples of how to calculate precise percentage of the deductibility for which you qualify.

## *IRA Phaseout*

| Single/Head of Household | | Joint Returns | |
|---|---|---|---|
| **Tax Years** | **Phase-out Range** | **Tax Year** | **Phase-out Range** |
| 2006 & after | 50,000-60,000 | 2006 | 75,000 - 85,000 |
| | | 2007 & after | 80,000 -100,000 |

## The Age 50 Catch-Up Provision

Since 2002 individuals who are at least 50 years old by the end of the tax year have a deduction/contribution limit that is $1000.00 per year higher in 2006 and later. Thus, a 50-year-old in 2006 could contribute $5,000 instead of $4,000.

A penalty of 10 percent, plus regular federal income tax, is assessed on funds withdrawn prior to age 59½. You cannot use your IRA for collateral since a loan is a premature distribution of IRA funds. If you become disabled and need your IRA funds, they may be withdrawn without penalty. Your beneficiary also has access to these funds, without penalty, upon your death. IRA contributions must be made by April 15 of each year, even if you get a tax-filing extension.

## *IRA Comparison*

| | Deductible | Non-deductible | Roth |
|---|---|---|---|
| 2005-2007 maximum contribution per individual under age 50 | $4,000 | $4,000 | $4,000 |
| 2006-2007 Catch-up | $5,000 | $5,000 | $5,000 |
| Contributions are: | deductible | non-deductible | non-deductible |
| Income tax treatment | 100% taxable as withdrawn | Amount over basis taxable as withdrawn | No tax if held over 5 years and owner is $59\frac{1}{2}$ |
| Withdrawals | 10% penalty pre $59\frac{1}{2}$ | 10% penalty pre $59\frac{1}{2}$ | contribution tax free at any time, 10% penalty on earnings pre $59\frac{1}{2}$ |
| Income tax treatment | 100% taxable as withdrawn | Amount over basis taxable as withdrawn | No tax if held over 5 years & owner is $59\frac{1}{2}$ |
| Withdrawals | 10% penalty pre $59\frac{1}{2}$ | 10% penalty pre $59\frac{1}{2}$ | Contribution tax free at any time,10% penalty on earnings pre $59\frac{1}{2}$ |
| 10% penalty exceptions | Death, disability, medical expenses exceeding 7.5% of AGI, equal payments, first-time home ($10,000), college | Death, disability, medical expenses exceeding 7.5% of AGI, equal payments, first-time home ($10,000), college | Nontaxable after 5 years: Death, disability, first-time home ($10,000) Taxable: Medical expenses exceeding 7.5% of AGI, equal payments, college |
| Distribution requirements | Age $70\frac{1}{2}$ | Age $70\frac{1}{2}$ | None |

An IRA rollover means that if you receive a lump sum payment from a qualified, tax-deferred retirement savings plan when you terminate employment or before retirement, the funds can be put in your IRA. You can roll these funds into your IRA without tax liability if certain conditions are met. Remember, IRAs are portable. They can be moved from banks to S&Ls or brokerage firms. After a transfer, the funds may not be moved again for one year.

## Roth IRA

The *Taxpayer Relief Act of 1997* created the Roth IRA, which is more flexible than the traditional IRA. Contributions are not tax deductible, but earnings and principal can be withdrawn tax-free at retirement. Under certain circumstances, investors can withdraw money (before age 59$\frac{1}{2}$) tax free and penalty free.

The tax-free nature of earnings from a Roth IRA means it seldom makes sense to make nondeductible contributions to a traditional IRA when that person qualifies to make a nondeductible Roth IRA contribution. Once again, keep in mind the maximum Roth contribution rate went up to $4,000 for tax years 2005 through 2007, and $5,000 in 2008 and thereafter. The increases parallel those of traditional IRAs as do the catch-up provisions for those over 50 years old.

## 401k

A 401k plan combines the attributes of an IRA and a pension plan. You contribute pretax earnings to a retirement investment fund. Your salary is reduced for tax purposes by the amount of the contribution and taxes are deferred on both the contribution and interest earned. The maximum contribution changes yearly, and withdrawal restrictions are similar to those for IRAs. Most 401k plans allow you to decide how much of your earnings, with certain maximum ceilings, you want to contribute and where the money is to be invested. A 403b or a 457 plan, like a 401k, is tax deferred and reduces yearly taxable income.

In 2005, the maximum annual elective deferral under 401k and 403b plans was $14,000. The limit increases to $15,000 in 2006. After 2006, the limit will be adjusted annually for inflation in $500 increments. There is an age 50 and older catch-up provision for 401ks. In 2006, if you are 50 or older, you can contribute an additional $5,000 to your 401k (in addition to the $15,000 maximum contribution). This increases the tax deferred maximum. This is a good deal if you meet the age requirements and can afford to make the maximum contribution. You may not make a catch-up contribution unless you have contributed the maximum to your 401k.

## Keogh Plans

Keoghs are retirement savings programs for the self-employed. You can be employed full- or part-time. You can contribute $30,000 or 25 percent of your earned income, whichever is less, to your Keogh plan. These plans can be set up by partnerships but not by corporations.

## Bonds

A bond is a debt instrument or an IOU. You loan your money to the government, a company, or a municipality and, in exchange, they give you a bond, on which they pay interest. The bond is their agreement with you. Some bonds, like U.S. savings bonds or Treasury bonds, are backed by the full faith and credit of the U.S. government. They are as safe as Uncle Sam's ability to pay. Some, like junk bonds sold by companies with poor or uneven credit histories, are a toss of the dice. Bonds, as an asset class, are usually not purchased for growth but for interest income. The interest rate should be substantial enough to attract you for a long-term investment.

You may purchase bonds in two different ways: as an individual bond or as shares in a bond mutual fund. There is an initial minimum investment required when purchasing an individual bond. If you are interested in purchasing a municipal bond, brokerage firms typically require a $5,000 initial purchase. Corporate bonds may require a smaller initial outlay, but these may still be prohibitive for the smaller investor.

## Bond Mutual Funds

In a bond mutual fund, you and other investors hold shares in a large group of similar bonds. Investment in a bond mutual fund achieves limited diversification in one asset class, and your initial investment is usually lower than when purchasing a single bond. Shares in U.S. Treasury bonds are sold through Government Bond Funds.

## Municipal Bonds

Legislation restricts what is, and is not, a tax-exempt government bond by defining categories of facilities qualifying for tax-exempt financing. Municipal bonds are sold by municipalities to raise money for local projects—airports, waterworks, and schools. They are typically free of federal taxes and, if you purchase them in your state, of state taxes. This makes them especially attractive for investors in higher tax brackets. Municipal bonds, although now somewhat less attractive due to lower tax brackets, are still a good tax-planning investment.

**General Obligation bonds**, the largest category of municipal bonds, are backed by the taxing power of the municipality issuing them.

## Corporate Bonds

These bonds are offered by corporations to raise the money necessary for a company's growth. Maturities range from five to 30 years and carry varying degrees of risk and interest. Purchasing a corporate bond guarantees that on a specific date, usually twice a year, you will receive a fixed interest payment. The principal is due when the bond is retired. Bonds are usually sold in $1,000 units and are purchased for income. Bonds may not always outrun inflation, but if you can lock in high interest rates, you will have a strong income source during economically stable and unstable times.

## Junk Bonds

Companies with poor credit histories or high levels of debt sell junk bonds. These are not investment quality bonds. The credit rating of many well-known corporations has been downgraded in recent years, and the bonds they sell are rated as junk bonds. A junk bond pays higher interest and represents greater risk.

## Bond Ratings

Bonds are rated alphabetically from the highest (AAA) to the lowest (D). The rating is more important than the company issuing the bond. The greater the risk, the higher the interest paid. Bonds rated BBB (Baa) or better are considered to be investment quality.

| Ratings | Moody's | Standard & Poors |
|---|---|---|
| Highest quality | Aaa | AAA |
| High quality | Aa | AA |
| Upper medium quality | A | A |
| Medium grade | Baa | BBB |
| Somewhat speculative | Ba | BB |
| Low grade, speculative | B | B |
| Low grade, default possible | Caa | CCC |
| Low grade, partial recovery possible | Ca | CC |
| Default, recovery unlikely | C | C |

## Stocks

If you own shares of stock in a company, you have an equity or owner-ship position in that company. Funds that buy stocks are often called equity funds. The company's individual performance, general economic conditions, and Wall Street sentiment all influence a stock's price movement. Buy stock for its price appreciation and/or dividends. The dividend is a dollar amount that a company pays its stockholders.

## Reading Stock Quotations

The following is an example of published stock quotations.

- The left column—YTD percentage change (Year to date percentage change) shows the price percentage change for the calendar year, adjusted for splits and dividends over 10%.

- The next two columns of numbers represent the highest and lowest price in the preceding 52 weeks

- The next column lists the name and trading symbol of the stock.

- DIV are annual disbursements (dividends) based on the last monthly, quarterly, semiannual, or annual declaration.

- YLD % (yield %)—is dividends paid as a percentage of price.

- PE (price earnings) is the closing market price divided by the company's per-share earnings for the most recent four quarters.

- VOL 100s is the unofficial daily total (volume) of shares traded.

- The final two columns indicate the day's closing price and the change in the price per share compared with the previous day's closing price.

| YTD % CHG | 52 WK HI | 52 WK LO | STOCK/Symbol | DIV | YLD% | PE | VOL 100s | LAST | NET CHG |
|---|---|---|---|---|---|---|---|---|---|
| -13.6 | 113.50 | 64.00 | Hitachi HIT | .71e | 1.0 | ... | 974 | 74.34 | -0.01 |
| -31.3 | 16.56 | 9.08 | Hollingrint A HLR | .55 | 5.0 | dd | 378 | 10.90 | -0.05 |
| +4.4 | 53.73 | 30.30 | HomeDpt HD | .20f | .4 | 40 | 108602 | 47.70 | +1.31 |
| +91.5 | 9.49 | 3.94 | Homestake HM | .03 | .3 | cc | 9065 | 8.02 | -0.18 |
| +2.0 | 27.13 | 19.96 | HonInd HNI | .48 | 1.8 | 21 | 876 | 26.00 | +0.20 |
| +4.0 | 92.35 | 54.59 | HondaMotor HMC | .41e | .5 | ... | 223 | 76.81 | +0.61 |

Stocks require management. Most people owning stocks, especially large blocks, do not easily forget their up and down movements. If Wall Street's fluctuations make you nervous, look for a more stable, long-term investment that requires less watching and worrying. Purchasing stocks is a calculated gamble based on luck, the economy, your knowledge, and of course, the dependability of your broker.

## Exchange-Traded Funds

Between 2000 and 2005 the money flowing into exchange-traded funds has grown dramatically. Exchange-traded funds, or ETFs, trade like stocks but look like index-tracking mutual funds. ETFs bundle together a selection of stocks, typically based on a well-known index. That selection of stocks is then marketed as one security just like a single stock. Its price fluctuates and, like a stock, it is traded continuously throughout the day. However, like mutual funds when you purchase an ETF, you are buying a selection of stocks, not just one, so you have some diversification.

In 2005, there were 143 different varieties of ETFs. They tracked everything from large benchmarks like the S&P 500 to different market sectors like pharmaceuticals, energy, and technology. There are ETFs that track geographic regions, countries, and bonds. Over the next year or two, plan on seeing the emergence of ETFs tied to a diversified basket of various commodities or hard assets. These could include precious metals, energy, and agriculture.

## *Exchange-Traded Funds / ETFs*

| Name | Symbol | Issuer |
|------|--------|--------|
| DIAMONDS | DIA | PDR Services LLC |
| IMidCap SPDRS | MDY | PDR Services LLC |
| Nasdaq-100 Index Tracking Stock | QQQ | NIPS Inc |
| Vanguard Extended Market VIPERS | XF | Vanguard |
| Vanguard Total Stock Market VIPERS | VTI | Vanguard |
| iShares Lehman 1-3 Year Treasury Bond Fund | SHY | BGI |
| iShares Lehman 20+ Year Treasury Bond Fund | TLT | BGI |
| iShares Russell Midcap Growth Index Fund | WP | BGI |
| iShares Russell Midcap Value Index Fund | IWS | BGI |

With many ETFs, you are buying market leaders in a certain market sector or index. The expense ratio of ETFs is usually lower than that of most mutual funds, and there may be more flexibility in how they are taxed. Most U.S.-based ETFs are traded presently on the American Stock Exchange.

| *Index* | *Tracks . . .* |
|---------|----------------|
| S&P 500 | the Standard & Poor's 500 |
| Morgan Stanley EAFE | stock markets in Europe, Australia, the Far East |
| Russell 2000 | smaller companies, small capitalization stocks |
| Morgan Stanley REIT | a composite of real estate investment trusts |
| Wilshire 500 | the entire U.S. market of about 7,200 stocks |
| Wilshire 5000 | large, mid-size and small company stocks |

Bond ETFs are based on the treasury index funds for one to three years, seven to 10 years, and 20 years. More firms will likely enter the market with bond ETFs. The lower expense ratios and liquidity make bond ETFs an attractive  alternative for fixed-income investors.

## Direct Stock Purchase Plans

A generation ago, investing in the stock market meant purchasing individual company stock. The problem was that high quality stocks are often too expensive to purchase multiple shares. There is, however, an alternative for the small investor wanting to own stock in market-leading companies. Almost 800 U.S. companies offer Direct Stock Purchase Plans (DRIPs) to shareholders. When you purchase stock directly from a company that offers a dividend reinvestment plan, you can reinvest your dividends.

Most DRIPs allow you to make optional cash payments to purchase additional shares. Buy high quality stock and continue to purchase additional shares monthly or quarterly. This allows you to use dollar cost averaging—you invest the same amount of money at regular intervals, buying fewer shares when prices are high and more shares when prices are low. Dollar cost averaging won't guarantee a profit, but a disciplined program increases your odds that your average cost will be lower than the average market price. This is an excellent strategy for long-term growth.

*There are more things in life to worry about than just money—how to get hold of it, for example.*

*— Anonymous*

## Mutual Funds

A mutual fund offers investors a diversified portfolio of professionally managed investments. Dollar cost averaging is also a good way to buy mutual funds. Mutual funds are sold in three ways:

**Load Funds** charge a 4 percent to 6.5 percent commission to purchase, plus an administrative fee of 1 to 2 percent.

**Low-load Funds** carry a 2 to 4 percent commission at purchase, plus an administrative fee of .75 to 2 percent.

**No-load Funds** may be purchased with no commission, but an annual administrative fee of 0.5 to 1.5 percent is charged.

## Fund Types

| | |
|---|---|
| **Balanced** | Invest in a mix of stocks and bonds |
| **Emerging markets** | Invest in stocks in countries with small but growing economies |
| **European region** | Invest in companies in Europe |
| **Global** | Stocks around the globe—foreign and U.S. Risk currency fluctuation |
| **Growth** | Stocks that should increase in price, focus is on future earnings potential |
| **Health/biotechnology** | Invests at least 65% in health care, medicine, and biotech |
| **Income** | Stocks/bonds paying dividends/interest, avoids risk by providing stable income |
| **Index** | Attempts to duplicate stock and bond market indexes. Strategy is buying the market |
| **International** | Foreign stocks, risk of political instability and currency fluctuation |
| **Largecap** | Stocks of companies valued at $5 billion plus |
| **Midcap** | Midsize companies with market value of $1 to $5 billion |
| **Natural resources** | Invest in stocks of natural-resources companies |
| **Pacific region** | Concentrates on companies based in the western Pacific Basin region |
| **Science/technology** | Focus is on stocks of science & technology companies |
| **Sector** | Invests in a particular sector/industry, does not offer typical diversification |
| **Small Cap Stocks** | Stocks of companies valued under $1 billion |
| **Value** | Stocks with low PE ratios, more conservative than a growth fund approach |

After purchasing shares in a mutual fund, you can redeem them at any time for their net asset value per share (the value of the fund's assets, divided by the number of outstanding shares). One of the most successful types of mutual funds has been a balanced fund. Balanced funds are a good way to diversify. They include stocks, fixed-income investments, and money markets.

Most investors considering mutual funds can use help in sorting through the numerous funds available and understanding how funds are ranked. The ranking of funds uses basic variables, such as price change over a specified period, but the combination of variables used differs widely.

When looking at the ranking of mutual funds, experts advise that you consider the following guidelines:

- Risk should be an explicit and important element in any ranking.

- Ranking should emphasize three- to five-year performance data. Shorter periods are less meaningful. Longer periods may reflect changes in management and/or philosophy.

- Rank funds against other funds with very similar investment objectives.

- Don't rely too much on rankings in your mutual fund analysis. Get a prospectus and annual report from top-ranked funds in the same category.

The summary-of-expenses table in every fund prospectus reveals the true cost of investing. All fee tables follow the basic format shown in the following table.

## Transaction Expenses
### Fees you must pay when buying or selling shares

| | | |
|---|---|---|
| Maximum charge | 0 to 6.5% | The commission (load) usually imposed on broker-sold funds |
| Maximum charge | 0 to 7.25% | Fee levied by a few broker-sold funds on automatically reinvested dividends |
| Deferred sales charge | 0 to 6% | Charge imposed if you redeem your shares within 5 or 6 years; typically, the fee declines 1 percentage point for each year you own the fund |
| Redemption fee | 0 to 2% | Charge paid on any withdrawals; usually expires within 6 months to a year |
| Exchange fee/transaction | 0 to $10 | Charge for switching from one fund to another in the same family |

## Fund Operating Expenses:
### Fees deducted, expressed as a % of average net assets

| | | |
|---|---|---|
| Management fees | 0.2% to 1.6% | Money paid to the investment advisor for managing the fund's portfolio |
| 12b-1 fees | 0 to 1.25% | Money used to pay a fund's distribution costs, including ongoing commissions |
| Other expenses | 0.2% to 1% | Ordinary business expenses such as legal, printing, and accounting |
| Total operating | 0.35 to 2.5% | Total of all the fund's annual costs expense |

## Index Funds—a Simple Way to Track the Market

Index funds are a simple way to *ride* the stock market. Whatever the market delivers in performance, index funds can provide. Buying index mutual funds is an inexpensive, tax-efficient way of buying broad exposure to the entire market or a particular market segment. Index funds are cheaper because they have no active management. These funds have been extremely successful. In the five years between 1993-1998, the returns of index funds tracking the S&P 500 beat 94 percent of the actively managed funds.

## The Background

Index funds have been in existence since the 1970s, but their phenomenal growth occurred in the 1990s. In 1990 the Nobel Prize in economics was awarded to Harry Markowitz, Merton Miller, and William Sharpe for their research into *Modern Portfolio Theory*, the philosophical basis for index funds. The theory suggests that investors will be more successful over time if they take a passive approach instead of an active, managed approach to their investing. Modern Portfolio Theory contends that trying consistently to beat the stock market is a losing game because of the expenses, fees, and taxes that are by-products of active, managed investing.

*The key to success is keeping your eye on those things you cannot see.*

*— Japanese Proverb*

When most people think of index funds, they immediately think of the S&P 500; however, you can buy index funds that track almost 30 equity and bond markets. There are more than 250 index funds. If you're interested in the non-U.S. stock market, seek funds that track the Morgan Stanley EAFE. If you're interested in small capitalization stocks, purchase an index fund that parallels the Russell 2000 index. Real estate stock investors who wish to own an index that broadly tracks a composite of real estate investment trusts would seek an index fund that tracks the Morgan Stanley REIT.

## Taking Action

Keep it simple. The simplest action to take, with the best chance of long-run success, is investing in index funds. What type of index do you wish to benchmark? Are you interested in stocks, bonds, or real estate investment trusts? Do you wish to mimic the performance of all U.S. stocks or only the S&P 500? The Wilshire 500 offers greater exposure to small, medium, and large companies than does the S&P 500. Begin by deciding which market, or market sector, you want to track. One fund may not meet all of your long-range needs. Consider mixing and matching two or three different types to achieve a balanced portfolio.

## Building a Foundation

After deciding your investment goals, time frames, and risk tolerance, it's time to look at an investment strategy. Look at the pyramid of investment as a pyramid of index funds. Those in the base provide a foundation. Experts suggest building your foundation on stock market index funds. Those that mimic the Wilshire 5000 index provide exposure to large, mid-size, and small company stock. It is broad-based and inclusive. This base is the foundation for investing in other types of index funds.

The upper layers of your pyramid should provide opportunities to branch out into small capitalization stocks, foreign funds, and bonds. A beginning investor might build the foundation with 60 percent in a fund tracking the Wilshire 5000, 25 percent in a broad-based global stock index, and 10 percent in a bond index. Monitor it occasionally, and let it ride.

## Show Me the Money

Keep in mind that all index funds are not created equal. As their popularity has grown, brokerage firms or commissioned mutual fund vendors have hopped on the bandwagon. Keep fees and commissions on index funds to a minimum, and keep a careful watch on the fees you are charged. The average index fund has an expense fee of .5 percent compared to almost 1.5 percent for a managed fund. But shop around so your investment savvy isn't limited to index funds. Investing in index funds is not a 50-yard dash; it's a long-distance run. It can, and will, provide winning results if you stay in the race and keep your eye on the finish line. No other strategy offers the same benefits, simplicity, low cost, tax savings, and performance.

## International Investing

The international stock and bond market permits you to further diversify. Anyone looking at stocks or mutual funds should also consider global investments. Many investment alternatives access worldwide markets, and a global strategy may enhance your overall investment plan.

Going global can be done conservatively, or it can increase your risk. Like the U.S. market, international stock and bond investments carry different levels of risk and reward.

|      | US Stocks | Developing Foreign Markets | Emerging Markets |
|------|-----------|----------------------------|------------------|
| 2000 | - 9.1     | -14.0                      | -25.4            |
| 2001 | -12.9     | -22.61                     | -2.37            |
| 2002 | -22.1     | -15.94                     | - 6.0            |
| 2003 | 28.5      | 40                         | 56.09            |
| 2004 | 10.88     | 20.2                       | 25.87            |

Note: In this chart, U.S. stocks are represented by the S&P 500; developed foreign markets by the Morgan Stanley Capital International MSCI EAFE index of major stock markets in Europe, Australasia and the Far East; and emerging markets by the MSCI Emerging Markets Free index.
Source: MSCI, Standard & Poor's and Bernstein

Look at how the investment has performed over the past five or 10 years before making a decision. A consistently strong performance usually indicates less volatility and thus less risk.

Although there are special considerations associated with international investing, including the risk of currency fluctuation, it should play an important role in most investors' long-term financial plans. The Morgan Stanley Capital International-Europe, Australasia and Far East Index (MSCI-EAFE) shows world market performance and the relative strength of most foreign currencies.

# Higher Risk Investments

The top section of the pyramid contains investments that carry the highest risk. You can design a well-diversified portfolio without ever entering the top portion of the pyramid. In this area, the potential for loss is usually greater than the potential for gain.

It is human nature to hear a tip on a hot stock and dump money into an investment hoping it will bring spectacular gains. Many of us want to start at the top of the pyramid looking for quick profits and fill in the rest of the pyramid later. It doesn't work that way! Use caution and common sense and never invest more in the top section of the pyramid than you would be willing to lose.

## Real Estate

Investment real estate is in the top section of the pyramid because of risk and the amounts of capital involved. This investment takes many forms: undeveloped land, vacation property, second homes, apartments, or office buildings. You can invest on your own or with others. There will always be demand for the right type of real estate. Will Rogers perhaps stated it best: *Invest in real estate because they ain't making it anymore.*

> *Do you want to eat better or sleep better?*
>
> *— J. P. Morgan*

In any investment, always be sure to look at tax liability implications. This is especially true of real estate. Tax law changes have curtailed many advantages that real estate investments had; although since 2003 the tax rate on long-term capital gains has dropped from 20 percent to 15 percent. Check with your accountant or real estate broker before investing in real estate.

Diversification is difficult with real estate unless you are affluent or take part in a limited real estate partnership. A Real Estate Investment Trust (REIT), most often sold through brokerage firms, provides management advantages and helps eliminate the headaches associated with managing your own rental property. Most REITs seek income instead of tax advantages.

## Precious Metals

Gold, silver, and other precious metals are in the top section of the pyramid. Price fluctuations can be extreme with these investments. Although gold and silver produce no income until they are sold, many individuals hold precious metals for the feeling of security they provide in unstable economic times.

## Stock Options and Commodities

Stock options are contracts to buy or sell shares of stock. The price of the option increases or decreases as the price of the stock increases or decreases. There are two types of options, calls and puts. If you think a stock will rise in value over a specific period, you purchase a call—the right to buy at a given price. If you think the stock will drop in price over a specific period, you purchase a put—the right to sell at a given price. All options have specific maturities from one day to nine months. If you limit your option trading to buying options, your maximum risk is your investment in the options.

Commodity futures are contracts to buy or sell commodities—corn, wheat, soybeans, etc.—at a future date. Price fluctuations determine whether you win or lose. Use caution. Stock options and commodities are at the speculative peak of the pyramid of investment. The New York Times reports that as many as 85 percent of commodity investors lose money on their buy or sell decisions.

# And Now What?

Remember the old days—the 1990s, when the stock market seemed to continually go up, often providing double-digit returns? Welcome back to reality! In 2000, 2001, and 2002, most of the world's markets retreated. Since then, many have begun  the long but uncertain road back into positive territory. Some people reevaluated their asset mix and decided to stay put, taking the long view that over time stocks will outperform other asset classes. Others sought the safety of fixed-income government bonds. Insecurity is more prevalent now. Navigating turbulent economic waters requires skill, patience, and a little bit of luck. Most people, especially those approaching retirement, have three basic concerns in tough economic times.

- Should I stay the course or dump stocks and mutual funds that have lost 25 percent?

- How long does a typical recession last? Give me some historical context.

- What can I do to preserve and protect my retirement income sources?

**Staying the Course vs Bailing Out.** Over time stocks outperform all other asset classes. From the stock market crash of 1929 through 2003 stocks returned an average of 10.3 percent. It's the length of that "over time" that causes some people concern. When the market crashed in October of 1929, ushering in the Great Depression, you would have had to wait 24 years for the market to return to its 1929 peak. In the recession of 1973-1974, it took seven years and seven months for the stock market to return to its 1973 high point. So everything is contingent on your time horizon—or how long can you wait?

Deciding if and when to sell a stock or mutual fund as it falls in value is very difficult. There's an old financial planning saying that if you find a stock interesting at $50, you're in love at $30 and married to the bitter end at $10. Selling is always harder than buying because we all tend to be loss adverse. We want to recoup any losses . . . often we simply can't.

There are no easy answers as far as when to dump the dogs. There are, however, some common-sense guidelines. Are the reasons you own a particular stock or fund still as valid today as the day you purchased it? Are the fundamentals still sound? Has the company or fund undergone management change, change in business strategy, increased competition, or a shift in market conditions? How have they responded? If the company fundamentals remain strong, and you are as comfortable owning the stock in difficult times as you were buying it, then trust your gut and hang-in for the long-run.

**How long does a typical recession last?** The general definition of a recession is two consecutive quarters of negative growth. The last two quarters of 2001 brought America into its first recession of the 21st century. The average recession lasts approximately 18 months. Over the last 30 years the depth and length of recessions has varied greatly. The reasons lie at the heart of what caused the recession in the first place and kept the economy in a recessionary cycle.

| Date | Event | Time to ... | Max. decline | Time to recover |
|------|-------|-------------|--------------|-----------------|
| 10/24/29 | Depression | 2 yrs, 9 mos. | -86.5% | 24 yrs, 5 mos |
| 12/07/41 | Pearl Harbor | 142 days | -20.3% | 341 days |
| 10/17/73 | Oil Embargo | 1 yr, 2 mos | -40.29% | 2 yrs, 3 mos |
| 10/19/87 | Stock Market Crash | 1 day | -22.61% | 1 yr, 3 mos |
| 08/05/90 | Gulf War | 67 days | -15.82% | 185 days |
| 07/20/98 | Global Financial Crisis | 90 days | -12.4% | 90 days |
| 09/11/01 | September 11 Attacks | 9 days | -5.7% | 85 days |

The public's psychology has a great deal to do with the length of a recession. Over 70 years ago, Franklin D. Roosevelt rallied the country with— *The only thing we have to fear is fear itself.* Indeed, public fear and the economic paralysis it causes is sometimes the biggest obstacle to overcoming a recession.

**What can I do to protect my retirement income?** Don't put all your eggs in one basket! Diversify, diversify, diversify. What was old news in the tech-heavy growth era of the late '90s has come back with a vengeance in the 21st century. Protect your potential retirement income by spreading the risk among cash and cash equivalents, bonds, and stocks. As you approach retirement, shift part of your equity investment into fixed income or cash equivalents. Begin this process five to 10 years prior to retiring. If loss can be defined as having to cash out at an inopportune time, then shifting funds toward more conservative areas before your retirement is prudent. That way you protect your future by reducing your risk at a time when you probably don't want to take as much risk. Do this gradually, it works better that way.

Keep in mind that most people will always want some money in equities. One rule of thumb suggests subtracting your age from 110. Thus, a 48 year old (110 - 48 = 62) should theoretically have 62 percent of his or her investable income in equities. Most of us don't plan on living as long as we will. For that reason, equities in whatever percentage you feel is appropriate should be a part of your retirement portfolio.

# Finding Someone You Trust

Trust is the single most important component in deciding where and with whom you place your investable income. If you wander into financial planning and the myriad investment options without much preparation or experience, trust becomes essential.

**What can you do on your own?** A few years ago a national brokerage firm ran television advertisements with the theme of investing your time before you invest your money. Too often we don't want to learn ourselves; we simply want to delegate. Investing your time by first learning the financial planning ropes makes you a wiser investor. If you know what investments are being selected and why, you have more input in changing your strategy for better performance.

Non-credit investment courses for the general public are offered by many local community colleges and universities. They are generic in scope and teach you the basic principles of cash planning and investment selection. Financial planning seminars are taught by brokers or planners in an attempt to develop a larger client base. Although they are sometimes forums for selling particular products, they can be helpful in giving you a broad overview of investments. If you prefer learning on your own, go to the library and read current books and magazines on investing.

**How do you find someone to advise you?** Set your objectives before meeting with anyone. Decide your risk tolerance. Assess how much money you want to keep liquid and how much you can invest. Establish parameters for how much yield and return you want your investment to provide. Then you are ready to find someone to advise you.

Seek people who have experience in the business and hold professional credentials. Does this mean you've got the best? No, not necessarily, but it does mean you'll be working with someone who has taken time to improve their knowledge and standing in their profession. Be prepared to review your total asset and liability picture. Don't be intimidated by the personal nature of the discussion. It is necessary that anyone helping you have knowledge of not only your objectives but also your investable amount of cash. The following designations represent different credentials in the investment community:

- A Certified Financial Planner (CFP) must have experience in the field, agree to a code of ethics, pass a comprehensive 10-hour exam, and have 30 hours of continuing education every two years. Some Certified Public Accountants (CPAs) are also CFPs.

- A Personal Financial Specialist (PFS) must be a certified public accountant, pass an eight-hour exam given by the American Institute of CPAs, and have experience.

- A Chartered Financial Consultant (ChFC) must have a minimum three years of experience in financial services (80 percent of the 25,000 ChFCs sell insurance) and pass 10 two-hour exams.

- A Registered Investment Advisor (RIA) must register with the Securities and Exchange Commission (SEC) and is paid to give investment advice. This title involves no educational or experience requirements.

**What kinds of questions do you need to ask?** When you visit an advisor, be prepared to interview them as much as they should be prepared to interview you. This is a relationship that should be built on trust, and the trust-building must come before any type of product discussion or sales takes place.

A potential advisor should ask you about your goals, your past experience with other financial advisors, your family situation, your risk tolerance, and your expectations for performance. They should urge that your partner be present since planning for two, done by only one, makes everything more problematic.

You also have responsibility as the client. Make sure that your advisor answers the types of questions you have for him or her. Here are some typical questions divided into three topic areas—background, philosophy, and feedback.

### Background

1. How long have you been a financial planner?
2. What type of financial designations do you hold? (CFP, ChFC, CPA, etc.)
3. How are you compensated?

4. Could you provide three or four references of individuals with income and assets similar to mine that I might call?

5. Are you active in any financial planning organizations?

## Philosophy

1. Do you favor one asset class or type of investment over another? If so, why?

2. Given my age and assets, have you established any model portfolios?

3. Do you favor mutual funds or individual stocks?

4. Who provides you with the investment advice you use when advising clients?

5. How much independence can I expect with regard to the investment advice I receive? (i.e., are there proprietary funds that you prefer?)

## Feedback

1. What kind of periodic feedback may I expect?

2. Will you be in contact with any of my other advisors—lawyer, insurance agent, CPA—to coordinate overall investment strategy?

3. How often do you suggest we sit down and conduct a thorough review of my asset allocation?

4. Will I receive written and oral notice anytime you buy or sell an investment?

5. What do you need to know about me?

**How can you be sure your money is in good hands?** You can never be totally sure. You can, however, educate yourself so that you are an active instead of a passive partner in your own financial planning. If you know what's being done and why, and have developed an open, ongoing relationship with an investment advisor, you are more likely to monitor your funds. If you have good communication with those advising you, the odds of sound investment strategies increase because you are both aware of the risk/reward relationships.

# CHAPTER 3

# Families and Law

*Which types of property ownership have survivorship rights?*
*Is probate a problem?*
*Should I set up a trust for my beneficiaries?*
*What is a living will and will it be honored?*
*Is just having a will enough?*

Y OU'VE PROBABLY SPENT A GOOD PART OF YOUR LIFE saving for the future and providing for your family's well-being. Protecting your family and distributing your financial assets and property, according to your wishes, are the most important reasons for preparing legal documents. This chapter addresses some of these often-neglected issues.

## Why Estate Planning?

Your estate includes everything you own—less everything you owe. Few people plan adequately for what happens to their estates at death. Lack of planning can result in higher taxes, higher probate costs, family arguments, and other financial or emotional costs. No estate is too small to benefit from planning. You may be surprised at how large your estate actually is after you total your assets—your home, insurance policies, cars, stocks, bonds, real estate, retirement benefits, profit-sharing, and stock-purchase plans. Anyone with income or property should do estate planning; it can save thousands of dollars in unnecessary costs.

Estate planning includes:

- accumulating assets
- preserving assets
- disposing of assets

An estate planning team often consists of an attorney, a life insurance agent, an accountant, and an investment advisor or bank trust officer. Using this team allows you, or your attorney, to develop an estate plan that covers not only drafting a will, but also tax issues, insurance, and investments.

## A Legal Planning Checklist

|  | Yes | No |
|---|---|---|
| 1. Do you have a will? | ☐ | ☐ |
| 2. Do you review it every two years? | ☐ | ☐ |
| 3. Does your spouse have a will? | ☐ | ☐ |
| 4. If you own a life insurance policy, do you understand its provisions? | ☐ | ☐ |
| 5. Do you understand the benefit provisions of your pension plan? | ☐ | ☐ |
| 6. Are your assets owned jointly? | ☐ | ☐ |
| 7. Do you currently have an attorney? | ☐ | ☐ |
| 8. Have you considered establishing a power of attorney should you be temporarily incapacitated? | ☐ | ☐ |
| 9. Have you considered setting up a trust for beneficiaries of your estate? | ☐ | ☐ |
| 10. Do you have a general understanding of how your estate may be taxed at your death? | ☐ | ☐ |
| 11. If you have remarried, have you made a new will? | ☐ | ☐ |
| 12. If you're contemplating marriage, have you considered a prenuptial agreement? | ☐ | ☐ |
| 13. Have you discussed estate planning issues with your parents? | ☐ | ☐ |

Estate planning should include provisions for your spouse and children at your death. A gift program can be established regarding personal property, residences, and specific bequests. Gifts to your favorite charities and any special considerations or instructions can be covered in your estate plan. Consider your retirement objectives, and make these goals a part of your estate planning.

Put documents in place now that clearly state your wishes. You may want to include telephone numbers, such as your pension and health plan administrators, the Social Security Administration, the IRS and your accountant, so survivors can get information quickly on taxes, required reports, etc. If you are a veteran, include the Veteran's Administration for questions about benefits.

## Wills and Power of Attorney

A will is the cornerstone of estate planning, yet more than two-thirds of Americans are without a will. Every man or woman, married or single, should have an estate plan, including a properly drafted will. Even if you and your spouse are joint property owners, each should have a will. It is planning for your peace of mind and that of your heirs.

Some people believe that, will or no will, your surviving spouse gets the estate at your death. This isn't always the case. Laws vary from state to state and in many a surviving spouse with two children and no will receives one-third of the estate and each child gets one-third. If there are no children, the spouse, in some instances, shares the estate with parents and siblings of the deceased. If you die intestate (without a will), your property will be distributed according to your state's laws. Your wishes and the needs of your heirs may not be considered.

> *Emergencies don't wait for you to get your legal house in order.*
>
> *— Anonymous*

Drafting a will most often includes the following steps:

- Naming an executor and alternate executor to handle property distribution.
- Choosing a guardian of underage children if you and your spouse should die.

- Setting up a trust fund for your wife/husband and/or children.
- Naming recipients of valuable (or valued) possessions.
- Designating charitable contributions.
- Considering estate tax reduction strategies.

Some attorneys will draft a simple will for under $300. This type of will usually leaves the entire estate to the surviving spouse. It is straightforward, uncomplicated, and should not take much of the attorney's time nor, consequently, your money. You can always make changes in your will if your circumstances change. Decide what you want in your will and then seek competent legal counsel.

A more complicated will leaves your estate to your spouse, with a contingent trust set up for minor children if your spouse does not survive. If your estate is large, and taxes could be a problem, a marital-deduction will might be a wise consideration. This will is written with a residual trust so some benefits flow to the surviving spouse. Assets are placed in a trust that should escape taxation when your spouse dies. The assets in the trust then go to your children or whomever you designate.

## A Living Will

A living will is a written declaration, directing a doctor or other health care provider not to apply heroic or extraordinary means of treatment for a terminal illness, thereby permitting natural death. The information must be precise, state clearly what you want, as well as what you don't want, for you to maintain control of your own destiny. About 90 percent of the state legislatures have approved living wills, and many local medical societies will send you a living will form free of charge.

## Tasks of an Executor

The tasks that an executor of an estate must perform may vary somewhat from state to state, but they will also have much in common. Many of the tasks will depend on what the will provides, as well as on the type of assets in the estate.

- **Preliminary Steps.** Locate and study the will. Confer with an attorney.

- **Assemble, Inventory, and Protect Assets.** List the contents of all safe deposit boxes; locate all property, real and personal; analyze business interests (whether to continue, liquidate, or sell), and arrange for interim management.

- **Study Financial Records.** Send death notification to all insurance companies, make a comprehensive study of the financial and business interests of the deceased in the years immediately prior to death, study employment contracts or any deferred compensation plans to determine whether or not payments are due to the estate.

- **Administer the Estate.** File federal preliminary estate tax notice; notify banks, investment brokers, and others of appointment as executor; close bank accounts and transfer cash to estate; inspect real estate, leases, and mortgages; have assets appraised; transfer assets to estate; file claim for Social Security or veteran's benefits; collect income, accounts receivable, and other funds owed the deceased or estate; keep beneficiaries informed of the progress of the estate settlement.

- **Determine Personal and Estate Tax Liability.** Estimate cash needed for estate settlement; select assets for sale to provide needed cash; file income tax return for the deceased; prepare for audit of income tax returns previously filed by the deceased; determine whether beneficiaries who receive property outside the will shall be required to pay their share of the death taxes; secure federal estate tax release so that distributions may be made as promptly as possible.

- **Distribute the Estate and Make Final Settlement.** In distributing assets from a residuary estate, choose a date that will result in the best tax treatment for the beneficiaries as well as the estate; prepare information for the final accounting, including all assets, income, and disbursements; secure releases from beneficiaries and, in some states, discharge from the court.

## Powers of Attorney

A **power of attorney** is a document authorizing another individual to act on your behalf. This includes taking action on any personal business that requires your signature or presence. The authority can be limited to certain areas or you may grant complete authority. That decision is yours. All states now provide that a properly drafted power of attorney will be effective even in cases of the disability or incapacity of the person who gave the power of attorney.

Some states have a **durable power of attorney for health care.** This is a death-with-dignity document similar to a living will, but stronger. This document authorizes another person to decide about life-sustaining measures to be used if you are in a terminal state. A power of attorney for health care takes legal precedence over a living will; however, some attorneys say it's best to have both to help ensure your wishes are carried out.

## Trusts

A trust is a way for you to turn over assets to someone else. The trustee (holder of the property) holds legal title and accepts all management responsibility of the trust for the  beneficiary. Trusts can be revocable or irrevocable. They can be established and effective during your life (inter vivos trusts) or at your death (testamentary trusts). Revocable trusts become irrevocable if trustees die or become mentally incapacitated.

Wealthy people have used the tax advantages of trusts for years, but trusts are also for average-income people who want the advantages a trust provides. Parents often use trusts to prevent immature young adults from rapidly depleting their inheritance. A trust may specify, for instance, that the inheritance be distributed in thirds; e.g., at age 25, 30, and 35. Trusts can provide an income stream for aged parents or charities. If you decide a trust may fit your needs, consult an attorney or the trust department of your bank.

A **living trust** protects your estate while you're alive and also can continue after your death. This is a legal arrangement that requires an agreement between you, the owner, and the trustee. The trustee can be a relative, a trusted friend, or a bank trust department; it can also be you, as initial trustee. The beneficiary of the trust can be anyone you designate. A living trust is activated while the owner is alive.

Under a will, an estate is settled in probate court. There are lawyers' fees and court costs, which can be substantial. The proceedings are a matter of public record, and substantial time can elapse before the estate is fully settled. A living trust, however, is settled without the cost and public nature of a court proceeding. A successor trustee distributes assets according to the instructions of the trust, with an accountant, notary public, or lawyer certifying any transfer of titles. The process is faster, less expensive, and more private. Trusts, like wills, can be contested; but a will is generally more easily contested by an unhappy heir than a trust. If you think the living trust might meet your specific estate planning needs, consult an estate planning attorney. There are two types of living trusts: irrevocable and revocable.

You cannot change an **irrevocable living trust** after it is established. The benefit is that it continues to be managed as you intended if you become unable to handle your finances.

A **revocable living trust** allows you to revise the terms of the trust as your financial situation or family needs change. The benefit of this type of trust is that you avoid probate, may possibly save on estate taxes, and you maintain access and control of the assets held in trust. Naming yourself as trustee allows you to continue to control your assets. The major disadvantages to a revocable living trust involve the time and effort required to transfer the titles to homes, bank accounts, securities, businesses, and other assets into the trust. Refinancing a home that is part of a trust may require removing the home from the trust and, after refinancing has been accomplished, transferring it back into the trust.

## Planning with Aging Parents

Like many people you may find it hard to think beyond the lifetime of your parents and harder still to discuss estate planning issues with them. Make things easier for yourself and for your parents by ensuring that they have the necessary documents prepared. If you have brothers or sisters, encourage them to be involved in these discussions from the beginning.

Help your parents prepare six basic documents:

1. A will that names a trustee or executor

2. Power of attorney

3. Durable power of attorney for health care

4. A living will

5. A letter of instruction to heirs

6. An inventory of finances

Organize financial records and information that you'll need when your parents can no longer make decisions for themselves. These are important issues for you to consider in possibly caring for an aging parent sometime in the future.

## Prenuptial Agreements

More than 50 percent of all marriages now end in divorce. With this in mind, more and more people consider a prenuptial agreement essential. There are three basic reasons for a prenuptial agreement:

1. To protect the estate of a previous spouse and/or children in case of death

2. To protect assets of the wealthier spouse in case of divorce

3. To set special financial conditions of the marriage

A prenuptial agreement can reduce family tension surrounding an anticipated second marriage. With such an agreement, neither family needs to worry about how that marriage will affect the inheritance of an estate. It also permits couples to accurately and fairly assess property and financial issues should the marriage dissolve. Many states now set a minimum on the percentage of an estate a spouse must inherit, but proper drafting of a prenuptial agreement allows many to avoid this regulation.

These issues should be included in any prenuptial agreement:

- **Estate rights**. Decide the minimum amount of assets to be bequeathed by each spouse to the other in event of death.

- **Income, assets, and debts.** Make full disclosure of all income, assets owned, and debts owed.

- **Assets.** Decide which assets will be in your name, which assets will be in your spouse's name, and which assets will be held jointly.

- **Divorce.** Decide who will pay the bills for necessities—rent, mortgage, food, utilities, and luxuries. Decide about separate property assets held before the marriage, and marital property assets acquired during the marriage.

- **Length.** Decide on the length the agreement will remain valid (usually five to 10 years unless renewed).

A prenuptial agreement should be negotiated several months before marriage or remarriage. Each person involved should have his/her attorney and accountant, and each should pay his/her legal fees. Establish your priorities—assets, lifestyle, property, children from previous marriages, etc. Make sure you will be restored to your premarital state of living in the event of a divorce. Ask questions and be sure you are aware of the divorce and inheritance laws in your state before you waive any rights. These are areas of potential conflict, and resolving them at the beginning leaves you and your partner free to concentrate on other aspects of the relationship.

## Property Ownership

**Joint tenancy** is ownership of property by two or more people with survivorship rights. Two or more persons may hold title to property in equal, undivided shares. When one owner dies, his or her share of the property is not passed on according to a will, but automatically becomes the property of the surviving joint tenant(s). If you and I own property as joint tenants, and I die, my interest automatically goes to you, my survivor.

When husband and wife jointly own property, it is called **tenants by the entireties**. This form of ownership exists only between husband and wife. Upon the death of either joint owner, the survivor automatically becomes the owner.

When property is owned by two or more people without the right of survivorship, it is called **tenancy in common**. Two or more people own property, each is the sole owner of his or her share. Upon one owner's death, the property is a part of that estate and can be passed on by will, or under state law if there is no will. Tenancy in common does not establish a survivorship interest as joint tenancy does. If you and I own property as tenants in common, and I die, my interest in the property goes to my estate, not to you.

Joint ownership is an unwise substitute for a will. When husband and wife place substantial sums in joint ownership, estate taxes may be needlessly expensive, and property can possibly go to unintended heirs. Without a valid will, an estate must be distributed according to state laws; therefore, check with your attorney about the laws in your state.

## Estate Taxes

Federal estate tax is paid by beneficiaries on inherited assets. The tax is applied to all property owned at a person's death and even certain property transferred during one's lifetime. The *2001 Tax Relief Act* lasts only until 2010. Currently there is no federal estate tax, or gift tax, on estates of one million or less. New exemption limits (from one million up to 3.5 million in 2009) and rate decreases (from 50 percent in 2002 down to 45 percent in 2009) will be phased in. Taxable estates can be reduced by the marital deduction, which lets an individual leave any amount of property to a spouse, tax free, avoiding the estate tax until the death of the surviving spouse. This may, however, increase the tax paid on the second estate.

The assets of an estate can be reduced with a lifetime gift program. By law, in 2005, you can give each heir up to $11,000, tax free, each year. Your spouse also can give up to $11,000, for a total of $22,000 to any heir each year with no gift tax ramifications. In addition, you may also exclude sums paid directly to educational institutions for tuition or to a medical facility for health care.

| Year | Estate Tax Limit | Tax Rate | Gift Tax Limit | Tax Rate* |
|------|------------------|----------|----------------|-----------|
| 2004/2005 | 1.5 million | 48% | 1.0 million | 35% |
| 2006-2008 | 2.0 million | 46% | 1.0 million | 35% |
| 2009 | 3.5 million | 45% | 1.0 million | 35% |
| 2010 | **scheduled to be repealed** | | 1.0 million | 35% |
| 2011 | 1.0 million | 55% | 1.0 million | 35% |

* The gift tax rate is equal to the highest income tax rate in effect for the year in which the gift is made. Currently that is 35 percent.

Attached to the "repeal" of the estate tax is the return of a capital gains tax on inherited property—a way to pay for the cost to the U.S. Treasury of lowering the federal estate tax. Instead of having their own estate tax, many states impose a so-called "sponge" estate tax. This allows the state to take advantage of the maximum amount that otherwise would be paid in federal estate taxes.

The new act repeals the state death tax credit in 2005, depriving states of that tax revenue. This will add to the revenue problems already facing most states due to the economic slowdown and could result in state legislatures deciding to enact their own state inheritance taxes.

Since provisions in the 2001 Tax Relief Act are scheduled to be rescinded, the law represents a "moving target." Currently, the strategies being most widely applied focus on flexibility and the willingness to consider disclaimers and other postmortem techniques. Except for the rare instances when a taxpayer is able to predict his or her own death, it is no longer possible for tax advisors to provide clear estimates of the taxes that will be due—on even modest wealth.

If you expect to pass on a larger estate, consult an attorney specializing in tax and estate planning. It makes sense to spend a little money on advice now to avoid a potentially large tax burden for your heirs.

## Learning More . . .

To find out more about the laws in your state, visit the law library at your county courthouse. You can also go to the world's largest law library . . . the Internet. If you have a question about how trusts work or real estate law in your state, there's plenty of information on the web. Be aware that laws are different in every state, particularly real estate laws. Doing legal research on the Internet is fine. If you are looking for free legal advice, however, beware. Even when you find an answer to a question, it's a good idea to look at more than one site to be sure answers agree. Look for a name behind the web address and information on who is writing the articles or running the site. Look for when the information was updated to be sure the information is current. Laws change; what is correct today may not be valid tomorrow.

One of the largest Internet legal sites, findlaw.com, has links to commercial and institutional sites, including bar associations for every state. The American Bar Association's site, abanet.org, has links to local bar associations and a directory of lawyers. The site lawguru.com has links to statutes, the Constitution, and other legal sites for every state and territory, along with a password-protected search engine. User-friendly explanations of basic legal issues are given on freeadvice.com, which also has *I want a lawyer* links under each heading.

The Internet is a great place to begin learning and to collect preliminary advice. As with financial advice, you should invest your time before you invest your money. It is one thing to buy the latest toy for your child online, and quite another to prepare legal documents online. There is wide variation in the quality of web sites on the Internet. The Internet gives equal billing to law libraries and ambulance chasers. Choose carefully and remember, an Internet advisor probably won't be able to argue for you in court if it becomes necessary.

## Common Legal Terms

**Administrator:** An individual or trust institution appointed by a court to settle the estate of a person who has died without leaving a valid will.

**Amortization:** The process of extinguishing a debt, e.g., a mortgage. Your loan payment consists of two portions: one applied to the principal and the other applied to the interest. As the loan balance decreases, the amount applied to interest also decreases and the amount applied to the principal increases so the loan is paid off, or amortized.

**Codicil:** An amendment/supplement to a will, requiring execution with the same formality.

**Common Trust Fund:** A fund maintained by a bank solely for the collective investment and reinvestment of the assets of numerous small trusts.

**Contingency:** A condition that must be met before a contract is legally binding.

**Corpus:** The principal body (capital) of an estate, as distinguished from the income.

**Custodian:** Person who controls an asset gifted to a minor under the Uniform Transfers to Minors Act. The custodian may only use the asset for the benefit of the minor, and the minor is entitled to take over control at age 21.

**Deed of trust:** Some states do not record mortgages. Instead, they record a deed of trust (essentially the same thing).

**Executor:** A person or trust institution named in a will and/or appointed by a court to handle the settling of an estate.

**Guardian:** An individual or trust institution appointed by a court to handle the affairs of a person who is physically or mentally incapable of taking care of his/her own affairs.

**Health Care Representative:** Your agent, usually a spouse, child, or other close relative familiar with your health care wishes, who can express those wishes to medical personnel when you are unable to do so under circumstances described in your Living Will.

**Heir:** One who inherits property due to blood relationship.

**Inactive Trust:** A trust in which the trustee has no duty except to hold title to the property.

**Inheritance Tax:** A tax on the right to receive property by inheritance.

**Insurance Trust:** A trust fund that provides management of life insurance proceeds.

**Intestate:** *noun*, One who died without a valid will; *adjective*, Having no valid will.

**Irrevocable Trust:** A trust which by its terms cannot be revoked (or can be changed or terminated only under certain conditions).

**Marital Deduction Trust:** A trust used to gain maximum benefit of the marital deduction by dividing property in half with a view toward having it escape taxation in the estate of the surviving spouse.

**Pour-Over:** A term referring to the transfer of property from an estate or trust upon the occurrence of an event as provided in the instrument.

**Power of Attorney:** A document authorizing an individual (or institution) to act as agent for another.

**Probate:** Method by which a will is proved to a court and accepted as valid. The process by which an estate is administered and titles to a deceased person's assets are transferred.

**Revocable Trust:** A trust which can be revoked or changed at any time by the person who established it in the first place.

**Testamentary Trust:** A trust established by the provisions of a person's will for all or part of what that person leaves.

**Trust:** An agreement in which one person or institution (the trustee) is the holder of the legal title to property (the trust property) subject to a legally enforceable obligation to keep or use the property for the benefit of another (the beneficiary).

**Trustee:** An individual or trust institution that holds the legal title to property for the benefit of someone else.

**Trust Estate:** All the property in a particular trust account.

**Will:** A legally binding declaration of a person's wishes in writing regarding matters to be attended to after his death (usually relating to property) and inoperative until his death.

# Your Healthy Future

*I never exercised before, why start now?*
*Am I exercising enough to help my heart?*
*Does my diet need to change as I age?*
*Does stress really affect my health?*
*My doctor retired too, how do I find another?*

YOUR HEALTH IS YOUR MOST IMPORTANT ASSET. Yet when people are asked what concerns them the most in planning for retirement, their number one response is money. Money will not provide much satisfaction if you don't have your health! This chapter addresses the key areas that promote well-being: nutrition, exercise, choosing a physician, and controlling and managing stress.

## What is Good Health?

In the past, good health was defined as freedom from disease or the absence of illness. The definition has expanded into the concept of wellness. Wellness is not only freedom from disease and resiliency when you are ill but also having abundant energy and leading a balanced life. Philosophers, psychologists, and theologians all have definitions of what a balanced life is. Most include having quality, relaxed time with loved ones while handling the tasks of daily living in a way that is comfortable for you. The emphasis is on taking responsibility for your own health. Delegating the task of keeping you healthy to physicians, hospitals or drugs doesn't have a part in the wellness concept.

59

Research shows the relationship between lifestyle and health. Altering your lifestyle to improve your health makes sense. If you have a predisposition to certain diseases because of heredity, then modifying your lifestyle or habits may decrease your chances of developing that disease, or at least lessen its severity. The choices you make regarding your health habits (exercise, diet, etc.) have the greatest long-run effect on the quality of your life. Chronic and degenerative diseases are slow to build and slow to manifest themselves. Protecting your health begins with acknowledging that there is a strong, clear connection between your lifestyle and your general state of health.

All of us are living longer, healthier, more active lives, often well into our 80s and 90s. The quality of those later years, to a certain extent, can be planned. Much of that planning must begin in your 40s, 50s, and 60s. Prepare now for longevity!

## Diets for Better Health

The National Cancer Institute recommends that you eat foods that provide 25 to 35 grams of fiber per day. Fiber-rich foods help promote a healthy digestive tract. To get more fiber in your diet, eat several servings daily of fruit, vegetables, peas and beans, and breads and cereals made from whole grains. Diets high in fiber and low in fat will help you to stay healthy.

Good nutrition means eating moderately and choosing a variety of foods for a balanced diet. Seven basic nutrition guidelines promote health and help prevent some diseases such as cancer, heart disease, and stroke:

1. Eat a variety of foods.

2. Maintain your ideal weight.

3. Avoid too much fat, saturated fat, and cholesterol.

4. Eat foods with adequate complex carbohydrates and fiber.

5. Avoid too much sugar.

6. Avoid too much salt.

7. If you drink alcohol, do so in moderation.

## The Food Pyramid

The American Heart Association (AHA) suggests the following guidelines for all healthy Americans over the age of two. These guidelines promote a wholesome eating style intended to reduce cholesterol to a level safe for your heart by controlling the amount and kind of fat, saturated fatty acids, and dietary cholesterol.

### American Heart Association Guidelines:

- Eat no more than six ounces/day (cooked) lean meat, fish and skinless poultry.

- Try main dishes featuring pasta, rice, beans and/or vegetables. Create low-meat dishes by mixing these foods with small amounts of lean meat, poultry, or fish.

- The approximately five- to eight-teaspoon servings of fats and oils per day may be used for cooking, baking, in salad dressings, or spreads.

- Use cooking methods that require little or no fat—boil, broil, bake, roast, poach, steam, saute, stir-fry, or microwave.

- Trim all fat you can see before cooking meat and poultry. Drain off all grease after browning. Chill soups and stews after cooking and remove the hardened fat.

- The three to four egg yolks per week included in your eating plan may be used alone or in cooking and baking (including prepackaged products).

- Limit your use of organ meats.

- Choose skim or 1 percent fat milk and nonfat or low-fat yogurt and cheeses.

- To round out the rest of your eating plan, eat five or more servings of fruits or vegetables and six or more servings of breads, cereals, or grains per day.

Research shows that eating cholesterol-rich foods is a factor in raising blood cholesterol. A diet high in saturated fat (characteristic of many, but not all, high cholesterol foods) is even more unhealthy. Limit or eliminate saturated fats, those solid at room temperature and the tropical oils.

Substitute mono-unsaturated oils (olive oil) and limited polyunsaturated oils (safflower). Fats, particularly saturated fats, can raise serum cholesterol. Food producers hydrogenate vegetable oils to make them last longer. This process creates trans fatty acids, which can raise blood cholesterol. Products containing trans fatty acids, e.g., stick margarine, can do as much damage as those with saturated animal fats, e.g., butter and meat. Low-fat and no-fat do not mean no calories. Health experts emphasize that moderation in all areas is the wisest practice.

## Food Labeling

The FDA labels grocery items to help consumers select healthier foods. Calories from fat are provided to help you meet dietary guidelines that recommend that you get no more than 30 percent of your daily calories from fat. A Percent Daily Value shows how a food fits into an overall daily diet and two examples show the ideal daily amount of fat, saturated fat, cholesterol, sodium, carbohydrate, and fiber, based on a 2,000 or 2,500 calorie diet.

Manufacturers previously provided nutritional information on a voluntary basis. The FDA has mandated that serving sizes be more uniform and more accurately reflect the amount an average person eats.

When you see key words and health claims on product labels, they mean what they say *as defined by the government.*

- **Light (lite)**—A light food must contain either one-third fewer calories or half the fat or sodium of its regular counterpart. Caution: some "lite" foods have increased sugar content.

- **Low saturated fat**—A claim of low fat is permitted only when there are less than 0.5 grams of trans fat per serving in addition to the requirement of 1 gram or less of saturated fat.

- **Reduced saturated fat**—A reduced fat claim is permitted only if there is at least 25 percent less saturated fat and trans fat combined and 25 percent less saturated fat.

- **Reduced**—Reduced-fat foods contain 25 percent fewer calories/nutrients than the regular product. (Cannot be termed both low and reduced.)

- **Good source**—One serving contains 10 to 19 percent of the daily value of a particular nutrient.

- **% Fat free**—Percentage must accurately reflect the amount of fat present in 100 grams of a low-fat or fat-free product. For example, if a product contains 2.5 grams of fat per 50 grams, then the claim should read "95% fat free."

- **Lean**—A lean food meets limits on total fat and cholesterol and contains 4.5 grams or less of saturated fat and trans fat combined.

- **Extra lean**—An extra-lean food meets the limits on total fat and cholesterol and contains less than 2 grams of saturated fat and trans fat combined.

- **Trans fat free**—A food that contains less than 0.5 grams of trans fat and less than 0.5 grams saturated fat per serving.

Nutrition continues to change. Guidelines for how foods can be labeled change. Release of a new food pyramid has been delayed due to different positions on what the precise recommendations should be. Questions about irradiated and genetically engineered foods and food additives are long-running controversies. If you want to know exactly what you are eating, you have to read labels carefully, watch the news for governmental and scientific announcements, and perhaps even do a little research on your own, or grow it yourself!

## Choosing Fitness

Why worry about fitness now if you haven't in years? Improving cardiovascular health, increasing strength, developing greater flexibility, lowering blood pressure, losing weight, increasing energy—the reasons are as varied as the numbers of those 55 and older beginning to exercise. Neighborhoods and shopping malls are filled with people intent on walking for fitness.

The *Couch Potato* study by the Cooper Institute looked at five groups, according to their fitness level. Not surprisingly, the least fit (most sedentary) group was the most likely to die first. Death rates from heart disease and cancer were the lowest in the most fit group. What was surprising was the huge difference in mortality between the least fit group and the second-least fit group. The death rate was 60 percent lower in men and 48 percent lower in women who were brisk walkers or gardeners, for example, than their sedentary counterparts. The American Council of Sports Medicine and the President's Council on Physical Fitness recommend 30 minutes of moderate exercise five to six times per week. Activity can be broken into chunks: 15 minutes walking to the store, 15 minutes raking the yard. The message is, just do it; get more active.

## Principles of Exercise

Always check with your doctor before beginning an exercise program. Select one you enjoy, that is easily accessible, and one you can stick with. In any exercise there should be a warm-up and cool-down period. Understanding the following principles will help you maximize the benefits of your exercise program.

- **Duration.** If you are healthy, a normal workout may range from 30 to 55 minutes in length after a five- to 10-minute warm-up. For maximum cardiovascular benefits, at least 25 minutes should be cardiovascular training. This means raising your heart rate to between 65 and 75 percent of your maximum exercise capacity.

- **Frequency.** It is usually recommended that you exercise three to five times per week, with breaks in between, to provide the best fitness training.

- **Intensity.** The amount of stress you place on body systems, including the cardiovascular system and muscles. A normal individual should stay within the 65 to 75 percent range for optimal conditioning.

- **Progression.** An effective exercise program is progressive. As fitness improves, increase your goals so you are adapting to greater exercise stress. Swim 10 minutes more or walk faster or farther.

Exercise is in! Most communities have abundant resources to help get you started. This is one area where anything you can do is better than doing nothing. Think about what you like doing and start there. As you do more you will feel better and find even more ways to increase your activity level.

Every person has a level of exercise activity that leads to cardiovascular conditioning. This level has an upper and a lower limit and is called the **Exercise Target Zone.** Count your heart rate for 10 seconds and multiply by six to find your resting pulse rate. Now calculate your exercise target zone.

## Computing Your Exercise Target Zone

|  | Example | You |
|---|---|---|
| 1. Begin with 220 | 220 | _____ |
| 2. Subtract your age | - 55 | _____ |
| 3. Result | 165 | _____ |
| 4. Subtract your resting pulse rate | -70 | _____ |
| 5. Result | 95 | _____ |
| 6. Multiply that figure by 65% | 95 x 65% = 62 | _____ |
| 7. And then by 75% | 95 x 75% = 71 | _____ |
| 8. Add your resting pulse rate to line 6 | 62+70 = 132 | _____ |
| 9. Add your resting pulse rate to line 7 | 71+70 = 141 | _____ |

The result is the heart rate range that is your Exercise Target Zone

**Sample Target Zone = between 132 & 141 beats per minute**

The following chart can be used to monitor your heart rate and assess your exercise progress. Every period of exercise should begin with a five- to 10-minute warm-up, after which you should again count your pulse for 10 seconds (no more), multiply by six and record your warm-up heart rate. Begin exercising and stop to determine your heart rate after five minutes, 15 minutes, and 30 minutes. Following your exercise period, calculate your heart rate again after a 10-minute cooldown.

## *Target Heart Rate Zone*

| Week | Resting | Warm-up | After 5 Min | After 15 Min | After 30 Min | After 10-min cooldown |
|------|---------|---------|-------------|--------------|--------------|----------------------|
| #1 | _____ | _____ | _____ | _____ | _____ | _____ |
| #2 | _____ | _____ | _____ | _____ | _____ | _____ |
| #3 | _____ | _____ | _____ | _____ | _____ | _____ |
| #4 | _____ | _____ | _____ | _____ | _____ | _____ |
| #5 | _____ | _____ | _____ | _____ | _____ | _____ |
| #6 | _____ | _____ | _____ | _____ | _____ | _____ |
| #7 | _____ | _____ | _____ | _____ | _____ | _____ |
| #8 | _____ | _____ | _____ | _____ | _____ | _____ |
| #9 | _____ | _____ | _____ | _____ | _____ | _____ |
| #10 | _____ | _____ | _____ | _____ | _____ | _____ |
| #11 | _____ | _____ | _____ | _____ | _____ | _____ |
| #12 | _____ | _____ | _____ | _____ | _____ | _____ |

The target zone is approximately 65 to 75 percent of your maximum exercise capacity. Exercise performed below 65 percent offers few, if any, conditioning benefits. Levels above 75 percent add little benefit and may be dangerous for some people.

If you are below your Target Zone, increase the intensity of exercise. If you are over the Target Zone, decrease the intensity by slowing your pace. As your cardiovascular system becomes more efficient, exercise will become easier, and you will need to increase the tempo to maintain your new Target Zone.

## Selecting Your Physician

Choosing a physician is one of the most important decisions you make. Most people select physicians by word of mouth. Others simply go through the yellow pages, finding a doctor close to home. Increasingly, however, patients are behaving more like consumers when it comes to choosing their medical care.

With more insurance providers turning to managed care, people are frequently confronted with a list of physicians they know nothing about. The first step is to understand your insurance plan by checking to see what options are available. Sometimes you can choose a physician who is not on the list, but your portion of the cost will be higher.

One source for finding qualified physicians is the staff of a university teaching hospital. Physicians on a faculty have already been well screened, and in all likelihood have outstanding professional credentials. University hospitals also often have referral panels of physicians who also serve as family physicians.

When choosing new physicians, you may want to consider:

• Background, where they attended medical school, any specialized training

• Type of practice and client base they have developed

• Fees and availability for evening and weekend emergencies

• Their participation in your insurance plan

• At which hospital(s) they have privileges

• The number of physicians in their practice

In a survey, physicians were asked to select the one factor that contributed more than any other to a good doctor. The overwhelming majority said taking a good patient history made a good doctor.

Most people want a doctor to take time asking and answering their questions. These personal touches become even more important as you age, and the likelihood of chronic illness increases. Communication is the key to a successful doctor/patient relationship. According to a recent study by *Consumer Reports* magazine, good communication contributes to better medical outcomes.

## Surgery—A Second Opinion

When a doctor suggests non-emergency surgery, you should consider getting a second, or even a third, opinion. This is not an expression of distrust in your doctor; it is standard medical practice. Most doctors want their patients to be as informed as possible about their condition. A second opinion can provide additional information to help in deciding if surgery is the best option for you. You have every right to that information. Some insurance companies require second opinions before they will authorize coverage of such procedures.

You can use several strategies to find a specialist to give you a second opinion. First, ask your doctor to give you the name of another doctor. Contact your local medical society or medical school for the names of doctors who specialize in the field in which your condition or illness falls. Call the government's toll-free number, 1-800-638-6833, to find out how to locate a specialist near you. If you are covered by Medicare, call your Social Security office. Many private insurance companies pay for second opinions. Contact yours for details. Medicare pays for a second opinion at the same rate as other services.

## Controlling and Managing Stress

We all age at different rates and often for different reasons. Events can age one more quickly. Look at the faces of the last three presidents before they took office and after leaving office. Stress can take its toll on anyone!

Some years ago, the *Journal of Psychosomatic Research* published a Life Stress Scale. This scale catalogs the events in one's life and their effect. Each event has a numerical value; the more stressful the event, the higher the value. Moreover, if you complete the scale and find the total number to be 150 or over within the past year, you could have a 50-50 chance of developing an illness.

There is major evidence that stress impacts physical health. High blood pressure, heart disease, arthritis, and certain types of ulcers have all been linked to stress. Experiments show that uncontrolled stress suppresses the immune system. With age, our biological regulatory mechanisms rebound less quickly. Stress-related hormone levels remain high longer in an older person than in a younger person.

## Life Stress Scale

| Event | Numerical |
|---|---|
| Death of a spouse | 100 |
| Divorce | 73 |
| Personal injury or illness | 53 |
| Retirement | 45 |
| Change of financial state | 38 |
| Death of a close friend | 37 |
| Son or daughter leaving home | 29 |

Source: Holmes & Rahe, The Social Adjustment Rating Scale

Over time, these elevated hormones begin to tax the system. The Life Stress Scale is a way to estimate the effect certain events will have on your health. If you have reached your middle years and are viewing retirement, you should have a good idea of how stress affects you. Stress is part of life, but you can have some control over it to minimize the effect it has on your health.

The stress-hardy person is proactive. He or she realizes that, in large part, our beliefs, attitudes, and current behavior determine our future. The stress-hardy person is not a victim who feels out of control, nor is he or she controlling. The controlling person believes that he/she is in control of his/her life, your life, everyone's life. The controlling person and the victim do poorly with change.

The stress-hardy person recognizes that there are some cards we are dealt (layoffs, illness of a spouse) that are outside our control. In those situations, the healthy attitude is to recognize that the situation is outside our control and then look for the hidden opportunities. When you do feel out of control, what can you do?

- **Health**—A healthy body weathers stress better. Sleep must be a priority and must be regular. Regular exercise lowers stress and improves the quality of sleep. When we're under stress, we tend to eat poorly. That's when it's particularly important to eat well to keep blood sugar levels even and to meet the body's increased need for nutrients.

- **Finances**—Getting control of our personal finances (reducing consumer debt, budgeting) is a great way of taking charge.

- **Relaxation**—Most of us know about the automatic physical reaction we experience when we are stressed. The other side of the stress coin is relaxation. Learn and practice relaxation. Relaxation improves immune function, muscular fluidity, sleep, and overall emotional health. There are many ways to relax: exercise, meditation, prayer, hobbies, music, etc.

- **Sense of Purpose**—It is crucial to know what's most important to you in the areas of family, work, friendships, and community. In order to reduce stress, decisions that we make (what we spend time and money on) must reflect our values and priorities.

- **Seek Support**—The definition of a support system: two or more people who know and accept you, and with whom you can be authentic; people who will provide practical/emotional support.

To be stress-hardy you must recognize that support doesn't just happen anymore in your communities or in the workplace. You have to be more intentional in creating it and nurturing it. Support is a basic human need.

Our lives change, and sometimes the changes are unexpected and unwelcome. Although change may be stressful, every transition presents new challenges. Many of us are familiar with the symptoms of stress overload—fatigue, changes in sleep and weight, aches and pains, particularly in the neck and shoulders.

Fewer of us have experienced stress under-load, defined as not enough stress or change. People need some stress to feel alive and continue growing. The challenge is to find the optimal amount of stress/change so that we feel stimulated but not overloaded.

## Techniques for Controlling Everyday Stress

Emotional and physical stress is part of experience. Whether the strain makes us susceptible to disease, or perhaps even to accidents, depends, to a great extent, on our attitude. There are no easy solutions to the problems causing stress. Here are a few suggestions for relieving the tensions of everyday living:

- Get out and cool off by walking, exercise, or physical work.
- Discuss stressful events with those you care about and seek their help.
- Rest or relax in a non-stressful environment—a complete change of pace.
- Be flexible, including modifying your own attitudes and behavior.
- Get enough sleep and rest.
- Avoid self-medication and have regular checkups.
- Balance work with play—loaf a little and laugh a lot!
- Analyze the causes of your stress and consider the solutions. Objectively!

Keith Harrell, in *Attitude is Everything*, suggests everyone can benefit from periodic attitude tune-ups. You can't control what happens to you, but you can choose how you react to those events—you can be in a good mood or a bad mood. By exercising those choices, you don't change the facts that stress, anger or disappoint you, but you can change the effect those events have on your body. Focus on a solution to your stress. By doing so you are more likely to stay positive, negate the effect of the stress, and begin a journey of finding solutions that may benefit you in surprising ways.

If you can learn to adjust your attitude, to cruise over or around setbacks, and to understand that even a good life is never perfect, you can put the power of an attitude tune-up to work for you. Your reward can be a better outlook, more inner joy, more strength, less stress, and progress in achieving the goals you have set for yourself.

## Staying Healthy

Good health is your single most important possession. Planning the years ahead involves staying as healthy as possible, so you can enjoy them. Some elements of good health are in our control and some aren't. If you have poor health habits it's never to late to change them. If you have a predisposition to certain illnesses because of family history, modify your lifestyle to minimize your risk.

Monitor your health with annual physical exams, blood pressure screenings, lipid profiles, etc. Ask your physician specific questions regarding your risk factors and what you can do to intervene . . . and then follow that advice.

The following brief health profile provides you, and those you care about, with an overview of your health history and current health status. After your annual physical, update your profile.

## *Health Profile*

|  | #1 | #2 |
|---|---|---|
| Date: | _____ | _____ |
| Date of Birth: | _____ | _____ |
| Height: | _____ | _____ |
| Weight: | _____ | _____ |

Currently Prescribed Medication(s):

_____

_____

_____

_____

| Blood Pressure | Systolic: | _____ | _____ |
|---|---|---|---|
|  | Diastolic: | _____ | _____ |

*(Blood Pressure: Normal 130/85; High Normal 130-139/85-89)*

Blood Profile:

| | #1 | #2 |
|---|---|---|
| Total Cholesterol: | _____ | _____ |
| HDL Cholesterol: | _____ | _____ |
| LDL Cholesterol: | _____ | _____ |
| Glucose: | _____ | _____ |
| Triglycerides: | _____ | _____ |
| Date of Last Physical Exam: | _____ | _____ |

List all Physicians and Specialists you currently see, include telephone numbers.

_____

_____

_____

_____

# CHAPTER 5

# The Tougher Issues

*How do I deal with my adult child who has returned home?*
*Will retirement put stress on my marriage?*
*Does it make sense to relocate, and is timing important?*
*My aging parent is more dependent now; how do I deal with that?*

DECISIONS OF THE HEART FOLLOW THE CYCLES OF YOUR LIFE. What are the tougher issues you may face? You may find yourself alone through divorce or widowhood. Your adult children may return, and you may face new parenting roles. As your parents age they will become more dependent, and you must try to meet both their needs and their expectations. You may relocate—new city, new home, new friends. Are you prepared for these tougher issues? Are your communication skills refined enough to handle these adjustments? Where will you find the strength and skills to adapt successfully to these changes?

## Flexibility and Communication

Life is richer if you live with flexible attitudes. Hardening of the attitudes can be as significant a problem as hardening of the arteries. Aging does not automatically bring inflexibility! Growing older can bring an understanding of life's cycles and patterns. As you age, you may become more aware of the quality of your life. You may better understand your limitations. Your friendships may take on a deeper meaning. Remaining interested, open, and flexible to what life deals is the key to enjoying living longer.

When you retire, time spent with your spouse will increase. That can cause difficulties. Each of you is adjusted to life without the other for a significant portion of the day. Readjusting to each other's needs and building a new life together takes effort. Awareness of the changes involved and the cooperation required is a major factor in making a smooth transition.

At or near the top of any survey on relationship satisfaction is good communication, including the following skills:

- Expressing thoughts, feelings, and preferences clearly
- Listening and hearing the concerns of others
- Negotiating effectively to reach decisions jointly

Are you accurately interpreting what the other person has said? Did you begin to formulate your response before your partner finished speaking? If so, you missed valuable information and responded to only part of what was said. After you listen and understand the message, check your interpretation with your partner. In intimate relationships it is extremely important to verify not only the facts of the message, but also the feelings expressed. Most of our misunderstandings come from our failure to check and make sure we have heard correctly. It is common to have been in disagreements that end several minutes (or hours) later in puzzled agreement, only to discover there was never a difference of opinion, only a difference of language and understanding.

*Experience is not what happens to a man, it is what a man does with what happens to him. It is a gift for dealing with the accidents of existence, not the accidents themselves.*

*— Aldous Huxley*

The ability to affirm others is rooted in how we feel about ourselves. If we are realistic in our expectations of ourselves and of others, then we are likely to be more affirming of others. We all have different skills and talents that develop in stages throughout our lifetime. Encouragement means accepting the level of accomplishment another person reaches and focusing on their effort. It means being more concerned that others believe in themselves than that they meet our expectations.

# Potential Personal Changes

As we age, our personal lives change. Relationships built over decades are comfortable; however, they may come under pressure as we redefine who we are and what we want out of life. Just realizing the potential stress that new situations will bring may help us as individuals and as couples to weather these emotional storms.

## Divorce

Although the statistics are alarming and disheartening, the fact remains that numerous marriages of more than 30 years end in divorce. Situations vary, but the one consistent element is that divorce is always painful. Even in cases where abuse or neglect is involved, there is a loss of the familiar, someone who was crucial to our identity. Divorce can be devastating whether it occurs after two years or 20 years of marriage. If you or someone you know is going through a divorce, there are things you can do to help.

Divorcing spouses cycle through different stages of denial, anger, and depression and for varying lengths of time. Healing and finding new direction will occur when the time is right for that person.

| *Divorcing Person* | *As a Friend* |
| --- | --- |
| Ventilate. Bottling up feelings just prolongs them. | Be available. Ask them to talk. |
| Consider reconciliation. | Listen. Hold the advice. |
| Allow your friends and family to listen and help. | Remain neutral. Focus on your friend's feelings and empathize. |
| Avoid blaming. The bitterness will drain you. | |
| Monitor your physical health. Eat and sleep regularly and maintain moderate exercise. | Socialize. Invite your friend to dinner and to social gatherings. |
| Seek professional help. Counseling can be useful in a transition time such as divorce. | Offer information. The name of a good lawyer or divorce mediation or a counseling center may be useful to your friend. |
| Give yourself time. Everyone responds and heals at their own rate. | Give them time. A divorce is a major loss in a person's life. They may cycle through many sequences of anger, depression, and acceptance. |

As partners cope with the emotions, they must also become aware of the changing financial conditions that are inevitable. Many of us know someone who died or divorced leaving a spouse with little knowledge of assets, liabilities, and plans made. Share this information. Planning cannot be done in a vacuum. Plan for life together and for life alone socially, emotionally, and financially. Becoming informed of the options available and the steps to be taken is the responsibility of each divorcing partner. For example, did you know that if you are divorced, have not remarried, and your marriage lasted 10 years you can file on your ex-spouse's Social Security record for benefits? You cannot receive both your own benefit and a spousal benefit. You will receive whichever is higher.

## Widowhood

As you age, the possibility that you may become a widow or widower increases. The average wife can expect to spend about 10 years in widowhood. Although no one is ever fully prepared for the loss of a loved one, planning while together can make the adjustment easier.

Planning begins and ends with communication. Talk with your spouse, preparing them for the possibility of living alone. Discuss areas that affect both of you. These include having an updated will, understanding your pension plans, and the necessity of financial planning. If you are eligible for a worker's retirement benefit from your own earnings record under Social Security, and the spousal benefit you are entitled to is larger, you receive a supplemental benefit to make up the difference. The total amount paid equals the larger of the worker's or the spouse's benefit. Become aware of the pension plan options offered by your employer or your spouse's employer. Awareness and understanding of the steps necessary to obtain benefits can lead to independence and self-assurance.

Studies of surviving spouses emphasize the importance of having the social support of two or more people who know you well, understand you, and accept who you are. Without social support, surviving spouses are more vulnerable to illness. You shouldn't count on your spouse as your sole source of emotional support!

As medical science devises ways to keep you alive on life support systems, it may be wise to discuss how you feel about this. Most states have living will provisions that permit you, in writing, to prevent the use of extraordinary means to keep you alive. Talking about dying, death, funerals, and burial arrangements is not easy. It is, however, necessary. Your wishes may seem obvious to you and fully understood by your family. However, if you cannot speak for yourself when a new option is presented for discussion, you will have to rely on the understanding your family has of your wishes. Such planning is crucial. It can lessen the painful confusion and the possibility of errors in understanding or judgment that can happen when you have to make decisions during times of great emotional stress.

## Boomerang Kids

How old were you when you left your parents' home and began living on your own? Chances are it occurred after high school, college, the service, or when you married. Today, adult children stay home longer and return sooner. Many young adults are delaying marriage and staying home into their late 20s and 30s. As you plan for life's transitions, it's wise to acknowledge that your adult children may be with you longer and more often than you envisioned.

> *There are only two lasting bequests that we can leave to our children — one is roots; the other, wings.*
>
> *— Unknown*

How you respond to this phenomenon is a personal decision. Many parents welcome delaying the empty nest. Other parents believe that guiding a young adult to independence is a parent's greatest gift and their greatest responsibility. The trick is to nurture an adult child from interdependence into independence.

An increasing number of incompletely launched adults are returning home to live for a variety of reasons. Many are simply delaying the responsibilities of independence and returning when financial and emotional hardships occur. The reason usually involves one or more of the following:

• **Economics.** Many college graduates are moving back in with mom and dad to save money as they look for a job or pay off college loans. It's easier and cheaper. With unemployment high, many young adults find they are underemployed. The skills and training they acquired in school are not applicable to what they are now doing, and/or what they're doing doesn't pay well.

- **Divorce.** In addition to delayed marriage, higher education, and high cost of living, the rising divorce tide is also sending adult children back home. Many times the reasons for returning home are not financial; they are psychological and emotional. Fifty percent of marriages are ending in divorce, and divorce often causes an adult child, and maybe even a grandchild, to need a place to live for a while. It's not inconceivable that you might help raise your grandchildren in retirement. After the devastation of a divorce, many young adults find the first step back to firm ground is a step back home. Most parents love and support a child unequivocally, and that safety net can be quite beneficial after a divorce.

- **Lack of Direction.** Dealing with an adult child's lack of will, purpose, and direction is a real challenge. One tough break or fear of failure can send an adult child back home. New and challenging experiences can be frightening. It's often easier to return to what you know, what you trust, and what's emotionally more secure. Setting goals and focusing on those goals can help young adults gain independence and self-reliance. Let adult children know that love and emotional support never stop, but that life transitions and independence are a part of adulthood.

- **Special Needs.** Our children are always our children, but for some parents, hands-on caring for a child doesn't stop with their adulthood. Special needs adults require parenting in all its facets, and it can become a lifelong duty of love and commitment.

How do you structure relationships with the adult children still in your home? This can be deep water for many parents. Our tendency is often to allow our adult child to lead a life that has all the pleasantries of adolescence with none of the responsibilities of maturity. If you have an adult child who stays longer or returns sooner, here are some practical guidelines.

- Communication regarding roles and expectations is a must. Sit down together and discuss these issues, including financial and household responsibilities. Responsibilities should be clearly stated, clearly understood, and agreed to by both parties.

- Collectively agree on how much financial help they might provide in meeting the mortgage payment or rent. Decide how they can help with grocery shopping, and discuss what evenings they might cook dinner. Let them know that their area of the home must be kept clean. These are adult responsibilities, and as adults, they must assume them.

- Let your adult children know that you have a parent's love and concern for them, but you will not monitor their social life or their social calendar. If they choose to stay out overnight, that is an adult decision. It is, however, their responsibility to let you know where they'll be so that you're not sitting at a kitchen table at 1:30 in the morning, wondering if they've gotten into an accident.

- Giving respect to the adult child and receiving respect from the adult child should be understood. Simply put—treat adult children as adults.

## Issues of the Heart

As people live longer (more Americans are living into their 80s and 90s), the issue of caring for aging parents will affect more and more retirees. Deciding how to care for parents in their 80s is also a part of retirement preparation. It is a topic most people avoid until it is upon them and then planning is not as effective. Address these issues now, developing alternatives and contingency plans. Discuss your plans and concerns with your aging parents while they are healthy. Then planning can be done jointly, with everyone's independence and everyone's input considered.

> *There are three faithful friends: an old wife, an old dog, and ready money.*
>
> *— Benjamin Franklin*

Discuss the future and the contingency issues: should they stay where they are or relocate? Keep the house or take an apartment or condominium? Talk about the need to update wills and organize key documents for easy accessibility in the event of an emergency. Clarify how you both feel about such topics as: what happens should you no longer be able to live on your own? How do you feel about moving in with us? Is a shared arrangement possible with another family member? These issues are not easy to discuss. They are, however, some of the most important issues and represent planning at its most personal level—planning for the needs of loved ones.

According to sociologists, the care of aging parents in this country is still being provided overwhelmingly by their own children, usually women. The elder care issue worked its way to the top of the corporate benefits priority list in the 1990s. There is a growing trend to create corporate policies that allow a better balance of family and career, including policies of support for employees caring for their aging parents. The Family and Medical Leave Act of 1993 provides employees with unpaid leave to care for family members with serious illness. This offers relief to employees who are working and also trying to care for their aging parents. These responsibilities affect one-fourth to one-third of all workers.

## The Home Care Dilemma

As the numbers of elderly increase, fewer family members are available to support and care for aging parents in their homes. The families of older citizens are, unlike previous generations, more likely to be in the work-force. They might like to continue caring for their parents in their home, but the daytime hours pose a problem.

- **Adult day care centers** are filling this need, and the number of these centers is growing each year. The idea is to provide mental and physical stimulation for the aging so that they can maintain the highest possible level of functioning. Adult day care provides an organized, well-supervised setting for older people requiring supervision, but not a continual care facility. This also allows those caring for elderly individuals a break from the constant, and often difficult, task of meeting their needs. Many day care centers are affiliated with nonprofit community service organizations.

- Many options provide an older person requiring care more independence. Many potential patients, still very much in control of their faculties, can get along very well with **home health care**. They want to remain in their home in familiar surroundings. The cost of this option often compares favorably with that of a nursing home.

• A **household chore service** allows older people the independence of living alone, providing the advantages of regular cleaning and cooking services.

## Alternative Housing for Seniors

There are a number of retirement housing options for seniors. The degree of assistance needed usually determines the best living arrangement.

• **Independent Living Facility**—Facilities where healthy, mobile seniors live on their own with a minimum of assistance.

• **Congregate-Care Housing**—Residents live in their own units, but they share centralized dining and support services.

• **Assisted Living**—These facilities provide a room and meals, plus help as needed with bathing, dressing, getting in and out of bed, and protective oversight. They are also called board and care, catered living, supervised care, personal care, or residential care.

• **Life-Care Communities**—In exchange for a one-time entrance fee, plus monthly fees, residents get a guarantee of assisted living, personal care, and nursing care as needed.

• **Continuing-Care Retirement Community**—These living arrangements provide the same type of services as life-care, but the costs are unbundled, leaving the choice of how to pay up to the resident.

## Aging in Place

As you consider living arrangements with your aging parents, think about the option to remain in their own home. The healthiest way to age is to age in place. Aging in place refers to staying in one's home and bringing in support services as needs arise. Keeping your parents comfortable with not only their surroundings but also with the people and things that define who they are helps to keep them emotionally and physically healthy. Old friends, neighbors, and familiar faces help keep aging adults interested and involved. Church groups and civic groups, as well as educational, cultural, and recreational activities remain familiar and may become even more important in their lives. The community promotes independent living by providing a support system.

The complexities of aging in place fall not only on an aging parent but also on the children who often try valiantly to line up the necessary support services from a thousand miles away. How do you find someone to cut the grass in summer? Who keeps the walkway clear in winter? Use all the community and private sector resources you can find.

There is now a broad range of programs and services, operating in virtually every community throughout the United States, to help keep older adults functioning independently in the community for as long as possible. The Department of Health and Human Services provides links to resources (hhs.gov/aging) as does the Administration on Aging (aoa.gov). Most state governments also have departments on aging. Check the Internet for resources in your area.

How can you help your parents with this choice to remain where they are? Many aging adults are house-rich and cash-poor. If that is the case, there are several options that can be considered to ease the burden of home ownership on your aging parent. There is the reverse annuity mortgage, which places a lien on the property until your parent moves out of the house, sells the house, or dies. The purpose of this arrangement is to create income.

Another option to consider is the sale/leaseback arrangement, which is often between children and parents. Your parent sells his/her house to you, and then rents it back from you, the purchaser. Your parent then has a mortgage payment coming in, providing a continuing income stream, without property taxes, insurance, or maintenance to worry about. If your parent lives alone, they may want to look at home sharing or renting a portion of their house to provide both income and companionship. These are practical steps that can be considered to meet the needs and desires of your parents. Our challenge is to make it possible for them to age in place comfortably, where they want to be, in their own home.

## Selecting Nursing Homes

No one likes the thought of placing a parent in a nursing home. Horror stories abound regarding the lack of quality care available, the tremendous costs, and the hardships on patients and their families. These decisions are not easy because they are decisions of the heart. Most people don't plan until a crisis is upon them. Ignorance of what is available, coupled with guilt and pain, complicate decision-making. Over one million elderly currently reside in the 22,000-plus nursing homes found in the United States. That is a relatively small percentage of the rapidly growing age-75-and-over population. Nevertheless, the decision to place an aged parent or a spouse in a nursing home may confront you. If you already know what alternatives are available, your decision will be a more informed one. If the possibilities have been discussed, decisions will be easier.

Most people seek one thing above all else in their final years, and that is independence. If, however, none of the alternatives are suitable for your particular circumstance, then choosing a nursing home should be predicated on knowing the right questions to ask.

**When does a person need a nursing home?** The General Accounting Office describes a nursing home candidate as a person with the most severe personal care dependencies. This means the person needs help bathing, eating, dressing, etc. When a nursing home is needed depends on the patient and the emotional and economic viability of his or her family.

**Who can advise me in selecting the right facility?** An excellent source is a family member or friend of a current nursing home resident. They can provide key information on what the day-to-day experience is really like. The older person's primary care physician would be the first source of information, along with other specialists who may have cared for him or her in the past. Clergy and social service agencies can also help you in selecting a nursing home. In many areas of the country, private groups rate the quality of facilities in their area. Skilled-care nursing homes are more expensive and maintain more rigorous standards than intermediate-care facilities. The patient-nurse ratio is lower in skilled facilities. Intermediate-care facilities provide licensed nurses only under certain circumstances. Many homes have both intermediate and skilled facilities, and patients are assigned rooms, depending on the severity of their condition.

**What if we cannot afford nursing home care?** There is a lot of misinformation in this area! According to a recent American Association of Retired Persons survey, 79 percent of the population over age 60 believes Medicare will pay for long-term nursing care. It will not! In addition, the cost of long-term care has risen so dramatically that there is little or no private health insurance to cover extended nursing home care. Explore all the financing possibilities available. Most often, pure economics dictate your choice of an extended-care facility for your loved one. Most homes don't require money down, but availability is often a problem especially for higher quality homes.

Find out if the nursing home participates in the federal-state Medicaid program. This pays the cost for needy patients; however, there is a catch. Medicaid often pays at such a low rate that many facilities will seek out higher paying private patients. Some individuals, however, facing a situation with a loved one that is likely to result in a nursing home placement, will plan to qualify for Medicaid. In order to qualify for Medicaid, estate planning needs to be done within a certain time framework to be effective. Contact your county social services and/or an attorney with experience in Medicaid planning for specific information on qualifying.

**What about long-term-care insurance?** These policies are relatively new. Costs vary and are determined by age, health, and coverage. Make sure the policy is issued by a company that is in solid financial condition and is rated A or A+ by A.M. Best Company. When looking at this type of insurance policy, consider the following:

- Guaranteed renewability for life.
- Inflation protection—increases premiums by as much as one-third, but is crucial.
- Covered custodial care, in addition to skilled and intermediate care.
- Covered home care.
- Pre-hospitalization not required.
- Alzheimer's coverage is usually described as "an organically based mental condition."
- Paid benefits for four or more years.

Some life insurance policies offer long-term-care benefits, called accelerated or living benefits. A portion of the value of the policy is paid to the policyholder in the nursing home rather than to the beneficiary.

**What comprises a typical nursing home population?** The typical nursing home resident is an 84-year-old widowed white female with multiple chronic illnesses. This presents problems for prospective male residents. Men are often put on a waiting list since most rooms are semi-private.

**What should I look for in visiting a nursing home?** Check its accreditation and if local groups that rate facilities have rated it highly. When you visit the facilities, use an organized checklist to make sure everything you want to know about is explained. Both the American Health Care Association and your state office on aging can provide you with a checklist at no charge. Remember—plan for what you want to cover. Talk with residents. If possible, eat lunch there to check the quality of a typical meal. Check housekeeping procedures and inquire about activities and programs for patients. More importantly, speak with the administrator about drugs and their use in controlling patient emotional disorders. These are hard questions, but you need to know the answers. A second unannounced visit at night is often advised. This allows you to see the evening staff and judge them and the care they provide.

## Retirement Relocation

Where you live and why is part of who you are and why you are contented. At retirement, many people consider moving. Retirees today are younger. They use retirement as a transition to new careers. They seek a new life in a new setting. Even the age of people in retirement communities is getting younger. Retirees look for a warmer/cooler climate, a smaller/larger home, being closer to children and grandchildren, or moving to an adults-only community.

Regardless of your reasons, you should take your time in deciding to relocate. Make sure you are moving for the right reasons and to the right place. Make sure your health history and medical records move with you. Visit before you move. Relocation can be a thoroughly enjoyable experience if you take your time and think it through. We are all living longer and, hopefully, enjoying life more. You spent decades growing up, decades in one or more careers, you can take longer than a few months to decide where to spend the decades you will likely have as a retiree.

## Family and Friends

Strong emphasis should be placed on feeling secure and at peace in your location. In other words, are you emotionally comfortable in this setting? Your feelings could suggest it may be unwise to move if much of your life has been based around one location. How you define yourself is often tied to a home or land. Too often, the shock of leaving what you know causes anxiety.

|  | Yes | Don't Know | No |
|---|---|---|---|
| 1. Has this move been thoroughly and thoughtfully discussed with family members? | _____ | _____ | _____ |
| 2. Do you sometimes feel you are losing more than you are gaining by leaving family and friends? | _____ | _____ | _____ |
| 3. If your spouse died, would you stay here? | _____ | _____ | _____ |
| 4. Can children/grandchildren visit easily? | _____ | _____ | _____ |
| 5. If you're relocating to be near your children and grandchildren, have you considered what might happen if they move? | _____ | _____ | _____ |
| 6. Do you and your spouse agree on the location? | _____ | _____ | _____ |
| 7. Are you moving simply because your neighborhood has changed and former friends have left? | _____ | _____ | _____ |
| 8. Could you easily accommodate an additional family member should the need arise? | _____ | _____ | _____ |
| 9. Does the area offer chances to develop friends? | _____ | _____ | _____ |
| 10. Will you have the opportunity to pursue the same kinds of hobbies and other activities? | _____ | _____ | _____ |

## Affordability

Do you know whether you can afford to move? Accurately anticipating the costs of relocating is not easy. Flexible planning, taking your time, and exploring several alternatives can make your relocation smoother, less expensive, and with fewer surprises. The old adage of investing your time before investing your money holds just as true for relocation as it does for financial decisions.

| | Yes | Don't Know | No |
|---|---|---|---|
| 1. Have you assessed the cost-of-living differences between your present and proposed location? | ___ | ___ | ___ |
| 2. Will you rent first, especially during the off-season before you move? | ___ | ___ | ___ |
| 3. Are there differences in cost of services such as doctors, hospital care, dentists, etc.? | ___ | ___ | ___ |
| 4. Have you explored rental versus purchase of property in the new location? | ___ | ___ | ___ |
| 5. Are there differences in tax rates? | ___ | ___ | ___ |
| 6. Does geographical location take precedence over the residence you are considering? | ___ | ___ | ___ |
| 7. If you're considering a condominium or retirement community, have you checked on association, maintenance, and/or clubhouse fees, etc.? | ___ | ___ | ___ |
| 8. Do you plan to have larger rooms with more space for entertaining, or do you hope to economize on both space and maintenance? | ___ | ___ | ___ |
| 9. Are you aware of the financing options available in financing a home purchase? | ___ | ___ | ___ |
| 10. Have you explored the differences between property taxes, utilities, and insurance in your current residence and your new one? | ___ | ___ | ___ |

## Climate and Accessibility

A common wish at retirement is to go home, return to the area where you were raised or began your life as an adult. You may consider moving to an area that you have visited. You think you know these areas well, but approach with caution. Home has changed a great deal since you left. You may not recognize its roads or its neighborhoods. Vacation homes beckon to retirees but what about the other season: the snow in the winter or heat and humidity in the summer? Look at every region as if you know nothing about it; don't rely on travel brochures.

|  | Yes | Don't Know | No |
|---|---|---|---|
| 1. Will your spouse adjust well to this move and climate? | _____ | _____ | _____ |
| 2. Will you be able to be active year-round? | _____ | _____ | _____ |
| 3. Have you felt the off-season climate in your new location? | _____ | _____ | _____ |
| 4. Is public transportation accessible to you? | _____ | _____ | _____ |
| 5. Are grocery stores and shopping areas easily accessible? | _____ | _____ | _____ |
| 6. Are airports and major transportation facilities accessible? | _____ | _____ | _____ |
| 7. Are opportunities available for work if you choose to? | _____ | _____ | _____ |
| 8. Are physicians/dentists/hospitals accessible? | _____ | _____ | _____ |
| 9. Is your new location accessible to your children/grandchildren? | _____ | _____ | _____ |
| 10. Are you near a church or synagogue should you decide to affiliate in your new location? | _____ | _____ | _____ |

Take time to do your research. Consider the effects, both emotional and financial. Narrow choices to three relocation areas and list the pros and cons for each. Spend time discussing choices and don't make a final decision until all your questions are answered and everyone involved is comfortable with the decision.

# CHAPTER 6

# Social Security and Pensions

*Is my pension plan protected?*
*With all the politics, how might Social Security change?*
*Will I need additional health insurance to supplement Medicare?*
*How are my benefits affected if I return to work?*
*What happens to my tax-deferred savings plan if I change jobs?*

EMPLOYEES TODAY CHANGE CAREERS MORE FREQUENTLY than did previous generations. Increasing numbers of employees work part-time during their career or after they retire. These trends can affect future benefits. It's very important to understand where the money will come from to achieve your retirement goals. People usually have three income sources in retirement:

- Pension,
- Social Security, and
- Investment income or savings

## Social Security

At retirement, a sizable portion of your income may come from Social Security. However, Social Security was not intended to be your only source of income. It is meant to supplement your pension, investment income, and savings. It is estimated that 95 percent of all workers are covered by Social Security, yet many of us do not understand how the system works. Many people think Uncle Sam takes money out of your paycheck, saves it for you, and pays it to you in the form of a monthly Social Security benefit check when you retire. Social Security doesn't work like that!

Social Security is an income transfer program. Payments to participate in Social Security are called FICA taxes, named after the Federal Insurance Contributions Act. Each year you pay a percentage of your wages to participate in the program. A limit is set on the total FICA taxes paid each year. Employers pay a matching amount. Your Social Security deductions, and those of other workers, are funding the benefits of today's retirees. When you retire, your benefits will be paid by all those still working. Each generation of workers, therefore, funds a generation of retirees. It is a pay-as-you-go system that has changed dramatically since the first Social Security benefits were paid out in 1941.

## Maximum Annual Taxable Earnings

FICA payroll taxes are paid on all earnings up to the taxable wage base. This taxable wage base changes annually. The 1.45 percent of the 7.65 percent that comes out of your paycheck is paid on all earned income. There is no taxable wage base for the Medicare tax. If you earn a million dollars, 1.45 percent will be paid to Medicare. The following chart shows Social Security taxable wage bases and payroll tax rates.

| | FICA Payroll Tax* | | Medicare Payroll Tax | |
|---|---|---|---|---|
| Year | Wage Base | FICA Rate | Wage Base | Medicare Rate |
| 2006 | $94,200.00 | 6.20% | all wages | 1.45% |
| 2005 | $90,000.00 | 6.20% | all wages | 1.45% |
| 2004 | $87,900.00 | 6.20% | all wages | 1.45% |
| 2003 | $87,000.00 | 6.20% | all wages | 1.45% |

*Workers pay tax on income up to the wage base.

## Earnings Estimate

Your Social Security benefit is based on age and the amount of earnings reported for you over your entire working career. When you receive your paycheck, do you know how the payroll taxes were computed? Do you know what earnings and work years have been reported for you? The Social

Security Administration now annually mails a *Personalized Earnings and Benefits Estimate* to all working Americans, age 25 or over. Expect your statement 90 days before your birth month. Review the information carefully and report any errors to the Social Security Administration at 1-800-772-1213. You can also access the Social Security website, ssa.gov, to request an estimate of your future benefits, apply for a new or replacement card, get information on benefits programs, check cost-of-living-adjustments (COLAs) and current earnings limitations, and request an additional Statement of Earnings. Since wage index factors and national average wages change yearly, it's best to inquire before relying on any estimated benefit. If you have questions about your Social Security benefit, contact your nearest Social Security office.

## Computing Your Benefits

When your benefits are computed, actual earnings for past years are adjusted to take into account the changes in average wages since 1951. Your adjusted earnings are then averaged together, and a formula is applied to the average to get your benefit rate. This ensures that your benefits reflect the changes in your wages over your entire career. Before you retire, visit your local Social Security office to discuss more personal questions with a representative.

## Quarters of Coverage

Before any benefits can be paid to you or your family, you need a certain number of quarters of coverage, or credits for work under Social Security. A quarter of coverage is used to determine the amount of work you have. In 2006, you receive one quarter of coverage for each $970 earned. Each year that figure increases, and you cannot earn more than four quarters per year. Next year's projection for a quarter of coverage will be approximately $955. Those born in 1929 or later, need 40 quarters of coverage to be eligible for retirement benefits. That equals working under Social Security, paying into the system, for 10 years.

## Applying for Benefits

It is usually recommended that you apply for Social Security benefits 60 to 90 days before you retire. If you retire before age 62, wait until approximately three months before your 62nd birthday to apply. Age 62 is the earliest a worker can receive benefits, and at age 62 benefits are reduced. The reduction percent depends on your birth date. Full benefits are paid at your full retirement age. If you work past your full retirement age, delaying benefits, you will receive an additional amount for each year beyond your full retirement age up to age 70.

Many people opt to take reduced Social Security benefits at age 62, before reaching their full retirement age. It often takes several years to make up the difference between your age-62 benefits and the benefit you would earn by waiting until your full retirement age. If you have earned 40 credits, you can start receiving Social Security benefits at age 62 or at any time between age 62 and your full retirement age. However, your benefits will be permanently reduced based on the number of months you receive benefits before you reach your full retirement age.

For example, if your full retirement age is 65 and you begin receiving benefits at age 62, your benefits will be reduced by 20 percent. If you begin receiving benefits at age 63, your benefits will be reduced by $13^{1}/_{3}$ percent. If you wait until age 64 to begin receiving benefits, your benefit will be reduced by $6^{2}/_{3}$ percent. If your full retirement age is 66, your benefit reductions at age 62, 63, 64, and 65 are 25, 20, $13^{1}/_{3}$ and $6^{2}/_{3}$ percent, respectively.

## *Social Security Reduced Benefits/Delayed Retirement*

| Birth Date | Full Retirement Age | % of Benefit at age 62 | Delayed Retirement Credit |
|---|---|---|---|
| 1937 & earlier | 65 | 80.00% | 6.5%* |
| 1938 | 65 and 2 months | 79.17% | 6.5% |
| 1939 | 65 and 4 months | 78.33% | 7.0% |
| 1940 | 65 and 6 months | 77.50% | 7.0% |
| 1941 | 65 and 8 months | 76.67% | 7.5% |
| 1942 | 65 and 10 months | 75.83% | 7.5% |
| 1943-54 | 66 | 75.00% | 8.0% |
| 1955 | 66 and 2 months | 74.16% | 8.0% |
| 1956 | 66 and 4 months | 73.34% | 8.0% |
| 1957 | 66 and 6 months | 72.50% | 8.0% |
| 1958 | 66 and 8 months | 71.67% | 8.0% |
| 1959 | 66 and 10 months | 70.83% | 8.0% |
| 1960 & later | 67 | 70.00% | 8.0% |

The delayed retirement credit is the percentage of increase in your benefits if you delay receiving any benefits until beyond your full retirement age.

## Earnings Limitations

Each year Social Security establishes limits on how much you can earn and still receive full benefits. You don't have to stop working totally to receive Social Security benefits, but if you earn more than the earnings limit, and you are under your full retirement age, your Social Security benefits will be reduced by one dollar for every two dollars you earn above the limit. Earnings do not include pension amounts, investment income, interest, Social Security and veteran's benefits, trust fund income, annuities, capital gains, gifts or inheritances, moving and travel expense reimbursements, jury duty pay, and certain sick pay and realty income.

### *Earnings Limit*

| Age | 2006 Earnings | | 2005 Earnings | |
|---|---|---|---|---|
| | Monthly | Yearly | Monthly | Yearly |
| 62-64 | $1,040 | $12,480 | $1000 | $12,000 |
| 65+ | no limit | no limit | no limit | no limit |

*Source: ssa.gov*

If you continue to work after receiving benefits, you will continue to pay taxes on your earnings. What you pay is, of course, based on your income. However, working after you begin receiving benefits could raise your benefit amount later on. Your benefits would then be automatically recomputed by Social Security.

## Medicare Coverage

Medicare coverage is not always complete health care coverage. Medicare has two parts: Part A (Hospital Insurance) and Part B (Supplementary Medical Insurance). Part B is optional coverage, and you must pay a monthly premium. The premium in 2006 is $88.50. In 2007 the Part B Medicare premium will be increased for individuals with adjusted gross income over $80,000 and married couples with adjusted gross income over $160,000. The amount of the increased premims will be based on ranges of income and could increase the premium as much as 33 percent in 2007, 67 percent in 2008 and 100 percent in 2009.Home health care will be phased into Part B coverage. The deductible amount is $100. Medicare becomes available at age 65 even if you're still employed.

If you are between 65 and 69 and are covered by your employer's group health plan, certain provisions will apply to your receiving Medicare. If you continue working past age 65, you must apply for Medicare with the Social Security office; otherwise your application will not be processed until you apply for Social Security retirement benefits.

Beginning Jan. 1, 2006, Medicare will offer insurance coverage for prescription drugs through Medicare Part D for traditional fee-for-service coverage (Medicare Parts A and B) or through one of the Medicare Advantage plans (HMO, PPO, etc.). After the $250 deductible is met, Medicare Part D will pay 75 percent of drug costs up to $2,250 per year. Enrollees pay 100 percent of the drug costs between $2,251 and $5,100, and then Medicare reimburses 95 percent of costs above $5,100. Individuals who are not eligible for prescription drug coverage through their retiree medical, or who have company retiree drug benefits that are less comprehensive than Medicare Part D, should consider enrolling in Part D. If your drug coverage is at least as good as that offered by Medicare, you do not need to enroll in Part D.

## Taxes on Social Security

When you begin receiving benefits, those benefits can be taxed. If you are single and your income in retirement, from all income sources, exceeds $34,000, then 85 percent of your Social Security benefit is taxable as ordinary income. If you are married, the income threshold is $44,000. Income sources include almost everything—pension, Social Security benefits, investment income, rental property income, etc.

## The Future of Social Security

The clock is ticking for Social Security. The system Franklin Roosevelt grandly established in 1935 is approaching its 70th birthday. At age 70 it will begin to confront a huge group of baby boomers ready for retirement benefits. In survey after survey, workers under 45 doubt the ability of the system to provide them with benefits equivalent to their contributions. Can the system deliver and deliver for the long haul? That's the question.

When, or even if, Congress does act, the solution will likely be a combination of elements under discussion. In addition to efforts to increase the amount of money available, changes may include some combination of increased payroll taxes, decreased benefits, and an increased age at which workers become eligible for benefits.

Each year the trustees of both the Social Security system and Medicare update their projections on the health and solvency of the two systems. In 2006, the trustees estimated that Social Security will stay solvent until 2018 but be exhausted by 2040. Medicare's trustees estimated that the hospital insurance trust fund financed by payroll taxes will have to be tapped beginning in 2013 and will be exhausted by 2026. However, the insolvency projections keep fluctuating depending on the economic assumptions used in the calculation—more/less economic growth, higher/lower interest rates, higher/lower inflation, higher/lower hospital costs, and rising/falling unemployment.

Social Security is still a political football. Alan Greenspan, chair of the Federal Reserve, has said that either taxes will have to increase, the retirement age will have to be raised, or the benefits of future retirees will have to be decreased. His directness, while unpopular, lays out the limited choices facing Congress and the President.

Over the next three years some of Social Security's basic principles may change but they will not change for everyone. Older employees will, in all likelihood remain in the existing system. Younger employees will become part of a revised system. Since Social Security is currently the most important income source for retirees (40 percent of all income received by those over age 65) wise planners should investigate alternative funding strategies. Social Security and Medicare may ultimately remain solvent much longer than expected but no one can afford to bet the quality of their retirement on that expectation. *Hope for the best but plan for the worst.*

# Pension Plan Basics

Your pension will probably provide the largest part, but not the only part, of your retirement income. Understanding how your pension is calculated, its distribution options, and its estimated monthly or lump sum payout provisions allows you to plan more wisely.

The average retirement age in America is dropping. Today it's $61^1/_2$. The average 61-year-old male is now expected to live to about age 80. A 61-year-old woman is expected to live even longer. As people continue to retire earlier and live longer, many fear they will outlive their available funds. Financing the years ahead requires planning and astute use of the money you have. Today the average employer-sponsored pension is worth about $5,300 per year, typically in the form of an annuity.

## Summary Plan Descriptions

Federal law (ERISA) requires that your pension plan administrators give you, in writing, a Summary Plan Description (SPD). The SPD should be written in clear, understandable terms. It contains information on pension eligibility requirements, accumulation or loss of benefits, filing for benefits, and similar topics. Read your SPD carefully. It provides the information you need to determine how your benefit is computed, election options, and what the plan provides. Take an active role in understanding your pension. Knowing what you'll receive helps to ensure a more confident approach to personal planning.

## Types of Pension Plans

There are two basic types of pension plans, a *defined benefit* (DB) plan and a *defined contribution* (DC) plan. In a DB plan, the amount of your pension benefit received at retirement is determined in advance by the formula stated in the plan, but the amount contributed to the fund may vary.

In a defined contribution plan, the contributions to the fund are stated, but your actual benefit amount is not known until you retire. Each year you receive an account statement telling you the amount in your account. At retirement you receive a statement of the total amount. Employers contribute and invest money for their employees (plan participants). The funds accumulated for an employee, plus any interest, less annual administrative expenses, make up that participant's pension. Under some plans, such as 401ks, employees also contribute. As the length of your work varies, so does the total amount contributed to the fund. That is why the pension amount received at retirement is not known.

Today many DB pension plans are linked to Social Security benefits. At retirement you receive a pension benefit that is, to some extent, offset by your Social Security benefit. These plans are referred to as integrated plans. They integrate your monthly Social Security benefits and your pension. For instance, some integrated plans compute your monthly pension according to set formulas, and then a percentage of your monthly Social Security benefit is subtracted from the pension amount. The amount remaining is your actual monthly benefit.

## From Paternalism to Partnership

More and more companies are moving from DB to DC plans. Pensions, based strictly on years of service and salary, will become rare in the next decades. Defined contribution plans reflect market conditions and employee initiative. As more options are offered to employees in an attempt to reduce or share costs, a bewildering array of choices and decisions confront employees. They may not be prepared to take responsibility for planning their current and future (retirement) benefits. Many employees are undereducated about their benefits, employer tax-deferred plans, the impact of periodic savings, and the power of compounding.

| | |
|---|---|
| No employer provided pension | 52% |
| Defined contribution only | 29% |
| Defined benefit only | 12% |
| Defined benefit and defined contribution | 7% |

Source: Bureau of Labor Statistics

## Vesting

Pension plans usually require employees to meet age and length of service requirements before participating in the plan. Under most plans, you gain a year of service if you work 1,000 hours in 12 consecutive months.

This age-plus-service formula varies, but most often it is based on age 21 and one year of service with employers sponsoring the plan.

The length of service requirement or vesting formula (vesting = age + length of service) determines at what point you are entitled to a certain percentage of the accrued funds in your pension plan. When you are fully vested (100 percent), you are entitled to all the money in your pension. The requirement for being fully vested varies from immediately to three, five, or seven years.

## Pension Payments

When you decide to retire, you must choose the type of pension payment that best meets your needs. There are essentially three choices.

- The first, and most popular, is the **joint and survivor option.** With this choice, you receive a reduced monthly pension check, and your spouse continues to receive a pension check at your death if he or she outlives you.

- The second option is the **monthly annuity.** If you select this option, you will receive an amount monthly for the remainder of your life but your spouse does not receive any money from your pension plan. If you choose this option, both you and your spouse must endorse the decision, and in most cases the endorsement must be notarized.

- The third choice in some plans is the **lump sum.** You receive all the money in one payment, including the interest it has earned through the years. If you elect a lump sum payment, do your homework on how to manage it.

## Underfunded Pension Plans

The government watchdog on pension underfunding is the *Pension Benefit Guaranty Corporation* (PBGC) which insures the defined benefit pension plans of corporations. If you have questions about the funding of your pension plan, call the PBGC at 202-326-4000. You can also write to:

> U.S. Department of Labor
> Division of Technical Assistance and Inquiries
> 200 Constitution Ave., NW
> Washington, DC 20216

Request the publication *What You Should Know About Pension Law*. The *1997 Retirement Protection Act* closes the funding gap created by pension underfunding and requires employers to notify their employees if a pension plan is underfunded.

## Tax-Deferred Savings Plans

These are DC plans that allow you to contribute a predetermined portion of your earnings into an account, frequently along with matching contributions from your employer. These plans have become part of most pension plans during the last decade. They combine attributes of an IRA and an employer-sponsored pension plan. Their popularity has been fueled by exceptionally strong stock market performance. Projections show that assets held in DC plans will overtake assets held in DB plans.

There are two principal types of plans: a **savings and thrift plan** in which an employee contribution is matched in whole or in part by the employer, and a **deferred profit-sharing plan** in which the employer contributes a portion of profits. In most plans, you can choose your own investments.

These plans often permit employees to defer income and taxes. Your taxable income is reduced by the amount of your contributions. If you're making $40,000 a year and the 401k allows you to contribute up to 5 percent of your salary ($2,000), your W-2 at the end of the year will report taxable income of $38,000. You might, therefore, be in a lower tax bracket than if you chose not to contribute to the plan. Chances are that you will be in a lower tax bracket at retirement and your 401k distributions will be taxed at this lower rate.

In 2006, the maximum annual deferral under 401k or 403b plans is $15,000 (plus any additional over-50 *catch-up* provisions). After 2006 the limit will be adjusted annually for inflation in $500 increments.

### Payroll Deduction

Your contributions to your savings plan are usually deducted from your paycheck. Using payroll deductions provides the discipline to save. If you don't see it, you don't miss it! Most people at mid-career today probably won't have enough money to retire unless they save more now or work beyond the normal retirement age.

## Employer Contributions

Many savings plans have employers matching a percentage of your contributions. This is an incentive by your employer to encourage you to save and increase your self-reliance. You can borrow against the savings plan and pay yourself back, or take a hardship withdrawal if your situation merits one. But beware—any withdrawal (versus a loan) comes with serious penalties, and unpaid loan balances also result in high penalties and taxes.

## Portability

These plans are attractive because both your contributions and the earnings belong to you. Often, they can be rolled into another employer's 401k plan or an IRA if you change jobs. If you are vested in the plan, your employer's matching contributions and earnings also belong to you and can also be moved. You may leave the funds with your employer if you meet certain minimum balance requirements. Unless you have a serious and immediate need for cash, you should either roll the funds into another qualified plan or leave them in place.

# CHAPTER 7

# Second Wind Generation

*How do I market myself?*
*Will employers want to pay me less because I have a pension?*
*If I have a pension, should I accept a lower paying job?*
*Is age discrimination still a problem?*
*How do I network?*

THE DEPARTMENT OF LABOR DEFINES *OLDER WORKER* as anyone 40 or older. That's a protected class. Today age discrimination suits are the largest category of Equal Employment Opportunity (EEO) complaints. As our workforce ages, older workers will assert their clout. More importantly, organizations will become increasingly aware of the value that skilled, talented, energetic older employees bring to the table.

Will there still be age discrimination? Absolutely, but it will be less and less a factor in who is hired and who is retained. As we reach the middle of the decade, more of us will want or have to work after we retire. Some will start their own businesses, some will look for another full-time job, but most retirees will seek part-time employment. Welcome to working on—welcome to the second wind generation!

## Retirement Careers

Baby boomers won't retire. Not the way their parents or grandparents did. Recent surveys suggest almost 70 percent plan on working in some fashion once they retire. Much of this change is due to the economy. Stock market turbulence has eroded personal savings and investments. If your employer has a tax-deferred savings plan or a defined contribution plan, you've probably watched the value of your funds shrink. Those are the economic reasons to continue to work. The other reasons are just as important but have nothing at all to do with money.

Work for many of you defines who you are. Work gives your life structure, fulfillment, and meaning. Many of us take refuge in work. Our colleagues can be like a second family. Often the support this second family has provided for years . . . you may find hard to leave. If that's the case, work on.

The flip side of working on is how you're viewed by an organization. Are you too old and too set in your ways or is age a non-factor because they're really interested in your skills and experience?

An organization's culture largely determines how it views older workers. The last 10 years indicate that Fortune 1000 companies have taken a rather schizophrenic approach to this issue. On one hand, older workers cost more to insure, represent greater claims, and—so the stereotype goes—are more adverse to learning new skills, embracing new technologies, etc. If a corporate or public sector organization embraces, even quietly, these views, they'll attempt to weed out older employees using reductions-in-force (RIFs), buyouts, and downsizing under the guise of cost-cutting. The problem is they often throw out the baby with the bath water. An organization may have gotten rid of a few "retired on active duty" employees, but they also lose a lot of talent in the process. What happens then?

An older employee with specific skills can't easily be replaced by two 27-year-olds making half the salary. Companies sometimes decide it's in their best interest to rehire retired, skilled, older workers as consultants. The net effect is higher costs—the older, ex-employee is often rehired at a higher salary level and the short-sighted planning also means additional costs.

Postretirement careers are an integral part of planning for the next third of your life. Start planning while you are still employed. Lay the groundwork now. Begin with a self-assessment. Think about what you might really want in a postretirement career.

- Do you have to work or do you want to work?
- What have you always wanted to do?

- Do you want to work full-time, part-time, or do contract employment?
- Do you want to work for yourself?
- What do you want a retirement career to provide?

The next few questions ask what your needs are in a retirement career. Most of those needs are practical. A second career should also ideally provide the intangibles: enjoyment, making a contribution, and mental stimulus.

- How much will you need to make?
- Will you need health insurance?
- How important is a second pension or tax-deferred savings plan?
- How will working after retirement impact your Social Security?
- If you are married, is your spouse in agreement with your working?

The final section of this assessment deals with planning. Think of it as a rough To-Do list as you begin putting things in place for reentering the workforce after retirement.

- What additional skills or education, if any, will you need for your retirement career?
- How well do you interview?
- What type of network have you established to aid in your job search?
- Do you have a list of people who could serve as employment references?
- Are you prepared to deal with the inevitable rejection that accompanies most job searches?

## Staying Put

The simplest second career is to keep your first one. This is especially true if you enjoy your work, your coworkers, and the challenges. Is the organization aware of your worth? Not just your supervisor, or your supervisor's supervisor, but your coworkers. You know this. It's not difficult to assess.

Often an organization's culture will change, new people come in, but you should have a pretty strong sense as to whether or not you are valued. If you are valued and you are happy—stay put.

There is a caveat to this. Don't rest on your laurels. Stay abreast, or in front of, what's happening in your field. Make yourself a valuable asset to your employer. Don't give up responsibility simply because you feel you've paid your dues. Dues, in the eyes of many, never expire!

> *A ship in the harbor is safe, but that is not what ships are built for.*
>
> — John A. Shedd

Your value to your employer is based, not only on your work, but also on your capacity to develop and adapt. Take advantage of any training and/or tuition reimbursement programs your employer offers. Make sure these courses go into your employment record because your effort shows initiative. Ability is ageless.

## Launching Second Careers

Finding a rewarding second career—whether you are 42 and recently retired from the military, or 62 and ready to leave a corporation—is always based on a few timeless principles. Know what you want to do, pay the price, and then do what you want to do. It's the *paying the price* that trips us up. Many feel they've already paid the price. Now's the time to coast. Coasting won't get you much.

All career planning comes down to four steps.

1. **Assessing Your Past Experiences.** Inventory the skills you possess, both professional and personal, what you have learned from previous jobs, and your accomplishments. These often can form the basis of a rewarding second career.

2. **Evaluating Your Present Position.** Review your experiences and the skills you have built over the years. Examine your present career goals. How can these be updated or modified to enhance your future?

3. **Defining Your Career Goals.** Consider your present goals and objectives. What do you seek in a career? Do you want great financial reward? Do you need only a way to keep busy? Do you seek challenge?

What do I want? is the most important question you can ask yourself, but it may also be the most difficult to answer. Define both short-term and long-range plans.

**4. Strategies: How to Get There.** Once you know your abilities and your goals, you must select effective strategies to reach your objectives. To be effective, any strategy must also be flexible enough to accommodate the adjustments you will need to make along the way.

## Turning Hobbies into Careers

Hobbies can become full- or part-time careers. This is especially true in retirement because of the additional time you have to devote to things you really enjoy. Many retirees have developed hobbies into lucrative and rewarding careers. If you enjoy stamp collecting, coin collecting, or antique automobile restoration, there is money to be made in assisting others through teaching or in buying and selling to increase or decrease your collection. If you enjoy furniture restoration, perhaps you can sell your work. It all depends on your desire, your entrepreneurial spirit, and the support you have from family and friends.

## Contract or Part-Time Work

Part-time work is an excellent choice for a retirement career because it allows time for volunteer work, sports, or hobbies. In some part-time occupations, you can set your own hours, giving you great flexibility and control over your time. If you have chafed over your lack of leisure time but don't want to abandon working entirely, explore the many career options offered by part-time work.

Many retirees build flourishing careers as independent contractors. You can use the expertise you have gained from your working years to become a consultant or independent contractor. Remember that organizations increasingly are hiring contractors to provide knowledge and skills once provided by their regular staff.

Outsourcing has changed the way companies work. Any supporting part of business judged nonessential to increasing the core business revenues is a candidate for outsourcing. These include 401k administration, payroll, and health claims processing. These are areas to investigate if you are considering a second career.

## Networking

The job market can be broken down into the formal, or published, job market, and the informal, or unpublished, job market. The published job market (usually publicized through advertisements and agencies) constitutes only about 25 percent of all available jobs. Seventy-five percent of all available jobs are not advertised; they are found in the unpublished or *hidden job market*. How do you tap into this job market?

The best way to reach the unpublished job market is by talking to people. If you are considering a change—part-time, flex-time, or a complete career change—talk with co-workers, family members, and friends. Let them know what your interests are, and ask questions about their careers or their fields. Let them know about your professional objectives, your qualifications, and your target market. The more people who know your qualifications and availability, the better the chance that the information will get to the right person at the right time.

## Working for Yourself

The challenge of a new career and the knowledge gained from years of experience entice some people to start their own business. Working for yourself takes guts! The decision should not be made hastily. There are as many reasons for starting your own business as there are business owners. Working on your own can be exciting and it can be frustrating. In your own business, you often have to do almost everything yourself. You are challenged and stretched. You must create policies, devise programs, and set goals.

Ask for help and discuss your proposed plans with knowledgeable people. Seek out those with experience in related areas. After a careful self-assessment and a clear understanding of the risks and rewards, you will be better prepared to meet the challenge. Working for yourself requires both financial and emotional capital. Most experts attribute small business failures to undercapitalization. Money is important, but the emotional toughness to hang in there for the long haul is equally essential.

Loneliness, self-doubt, and being stretched in too many directions can drain your enthusiasm.

**How to do It?** Begin with a plan! Once you have decided to go into business, you must determine what you want your business to be, now and in the future. Ask yourself: What business am I in? What is my potential for personal and professional growth? Take time in answering these questions. Keep your projections realistic. Don't overestimate income or market potential and don't underestimate how hard you'll have to work!

**Financial factors.** It takes money to make money, yet everyone has to begin somewhere. If you don't use your savings to begin your business, a bank, savings and loan, or other financial institution may be your best source for capital. All lenders will want certain business and personal financial data. Develop a portfolio about yourself and your business.

Most lenders use the *Six Cs of Credit* to assess your credit worthiness:

**Character ~ Capacity ~ Capital
Collateral ~ Circumstances ~ Coverage**

**Seek advice.** Talk with as many different people as you can, always keeping your goals in perspective and your dreams in check. Colleges and universities usually have Small Business Development Centers that offer assistance at nominal expense. The Small Business Administration operates a volunteer division of retired executives (the Service Corps of Retired Executives, SCORE) that offers free help with any business problem. Contact people in related fields who can help you establish market needs and potential. Finally, there is a wealth of material available from the government and your local library.

## Balancing Work, Leisure, and Learning

Whether you are in your first career, a second career, or retired, enjoying life means knowing how to balance work and leisure. This is especially true when retirement replaces work. Men and women often define themselves by their work. Without proper planning, this strong identification with work can make retirement a frustrating experience. Richard H. Bolles, in *The Three Boxes of Life*, suggests that we move from almost all learning, to almost all work, to all leisure. He urges we find a balance between learning, working, and playing. Such a balance is necessary at all stages of life. Decide what is important to you, what holds meaning, and then find the balance that is right for you. In other words, keep growing!

## *Four Keys for Life Enrichment*

**Awareness:** Maintain an alert, active outlook.

**Flexibility:** Keep your attitudes flexible and forgiving.

**Independence:** Cultivate the ability to make independent choices.

**Expansion:** Develop new goals. Find projects with purpose and meaning.

# CHAPTER 8

# Your Federal Benefits

*What's going to change and how can I plan for it?*
*What are the options for withdrawing TSP funds?*
*How will my FERS Benefits impact my Social Security?*
*Is a full survivor benefit the smartest way to go?*

I
T IS IMPORTANT TO UNDERSTAND YOUR BENEFITS and what you are entitled to long before retirement. Often employees discover that their planning began too late and they find themselves pressured to understand choices and make decisions in a very short timeframe. If you have not begun to plan, you need to make it a high priority. If your planning is under way, you need to evaluate those plans and make any necessary course corrections.

The following questions come up most often as employees begin looking at how their federal pension and benefits will impact their future:

- What counts toward total service time (eligibility requirements)?

- What are my options for taking my TSP money at retirement?

- How will my annuity be computed and how are survivor benefits factored in?

- Can I estimate how much I'll receive at retirement?

- What do I need to know about carrying my life and health insurance into retirement?

# CSRS

If you are retiring under the Civil Service Retirement System (CSRS), you've witnessed a great many changes in federal benefits—the Thrift Savings Plan was introduced in 1987 and long-term-care insurance was rolled out in 2002. In 2005 a new fund was added to the TSP that carries the potential for higher returns for younger employees but will automatically shift to more conservative investments as those employees near retirement. As a CSRS employee, you are probably getting close to retirement. Understanding what you are entitled to under CSRS and the choices you will need to make are extremely important.

First, you should understand your annuity since that's the cornerstone of your retirement benefits. Next, you need to make informed choices about any survivor benefits you choose to  provide, as well as life and health insurance options. If you will be eligible for Social Security benefits you need to understand the Windfall Elimination Provision. Finally, you need to know your options in making contributions to the TSP now and withdrawing your funds later.

## When will I be eligible to retire?

To qualify for an immediate annuity (one that begins within one month after separation), you must meet the combination of age and length-of-service  requirements listed:

### *Optional/Voluntary Retirement*

| Min. Age | Min. Service | Special Requirements |
| --- | --- | --- |
| 62 | 5 years | None |
| 60 | 20 | None |
| 55 | 30 | None |
| 50 | 20 | Must retire under the special provisions for law enforcement officers, firefighters, or air traffic controllers. |

## Discontinued/Involuntary Retirement

| Min. Age | Min. Service | Special Requirements |
|---|---|---|
| Any Age* | 25 | Agency must be undergoing a major service reorganization, RIF, transfer of function, determined by OPM. |
| 50* | 20 | Must be involuntarily separated for reasons other than for cause on charges of misconduct or delinquency. Must not have declined a reasonable offer of another position in your agency for which you are qualified—not lower than two grades below your current position, and at the same tenure, work schedule, and commuting area. |

## Early Retirement

| Min. Age | Min. Service | Special Requirements |
|---|---|---|
| Any Age* | 25 | Voluntary Early Retirement Authority (VERA) issued by OPM |
| 50* | 20 | |

## Disability Retirement

| Min. Age | Min. Service | Special Requirements |
|---|---|---|
| Any Age** | 5 | You must be disabled for useful and efficient service in vacant, equivalent positions in your agency and commuting area for which you are qualified. |

\* Annuity is reduced if under age 55. Reduction is 1/6 of 1 percent (2 percent a year) for each month you are under age 55.

\*\* No age reduction

In addition, you must have at least five years of civilian service and at least one year of civilian service under CSRS during the two years prior to separation. If you retire on disability, you do not have to meet this last requirement.

### What counts as creditable service?

Creditable service is generally the time from your appointment to your separation. When you apply for retirement, your personnel office completes a Certified Summary of Federal Service (SF 2801-1) that includes all verified and documented civilian and military service. You will be asked to review and sign the summary. Make sure it is correct. If you feel you have additional creditable service, it must be documented.

## Can I count my military service?

As a general rule, military service is creditable, provided it was active duty and ended with an honorable discharge. Service before 1957 is included in the annuity computation. You receive credit for that time even though you were not contributing to the CSRS retirement fund. No credit is allowed for any retired military service unless you waive receipt of military retired pay for that service. You do not have to waive retired pay for awards based on a service-connected disability, incurred in combat, or based on age and service in the reserves. Social Security deductions were taken out of military pay for service after Dec. 31, 1956. You can't count this military time for both Social Security and your CSRS annuity without making additional contributions to the CSRS retirement fund.

If you became a CSRS employee before Oct. 1, 1982, and retire before age 62, you will receive credit in your annuity computation for your military time without making a deposit. When you reach age 62, if you are eligible for Social Security retirement benefits, your CSRS annuity will be re-computed to eliminate your post-1956 military service time. To avoid this reduction, you must make a deposit of 7 percent of your base military pay, plus interest, for military service after Dec. 31, 1956. **This deposit must be made before you retire.** If you make the deposit, your post-1956 military time will count for both your CSRS annuity and Social Security benefits. If you will not be eligible for Social Security benefits at age 62, a deposit is not required, and your annuity will not be reduced.

If you retire at age 62 or later and are eligible for Social Security benefits, any post-1956 military service for which no deposit was made will not be used in your annuity computation. If you became a federal employee Oct. 1, 1982, or later, and have post-1956 military service, you must make the deposit for that military service if you wish to use it as creditable service for CSRS retirement eligibility and the computation of your annuity.

To receive a record of your estimated military earnings, for the purpose of post-1956 military deposits, send a completed Request for Estimated

Earnings during Military Service (OPM Form RI 20-97) to the appropriate military pay center. Your personnel office will furnish you with the address. Attach a copy of your DD 214, or equivalent, to your request for each period of military service. When you receive the earnings statement, forward it to your personnel office for information on making the deposit. Deposits must be made directly to the employing agency and completed before OPM's final adjudication of your retirement application.

## What about sick leave?

If you retire on an immediate annuity, your service will be increased by the days of unused sick leave to your credit. Under CSRS, unused sick leave cannot be used for retirement eligibility, but will be added to your creditable service when your annuity is computed. For example, if you're age 55 and have 29 years of service and one year of sick leave, you must work another year to have 30 creditable years of service, but you will receive an annuity benefit based on 31 years of service.

- **Other Creditable Service**—Credit is generally given for both civilian and military service performed for the federal government.

- **Leave Without Pay (LWOP)**—You are granted credit for LWOP that does not exceed six months in any calendar year.

- **Part-Time Employment**—For eligibility, part-time employment is treated as if it were full-time service for all time between the date of hire and the date of separation. In computing your annuity, if the part-time service was performed after April 6, 1986, credit is prorated based on your part-time work schedule.

- **Deposit Service**—Deposit Service is service time for which retirement deductions have not been taken. You receive credit for service performed before Oct. 1, 1982, when computing your length of service and your annuity. You receive credit even though no money was paid into the retirement fund. Your annuity is reduced if you choose not to repay the amount withheld, plus interest. The reduction is 10 percent of the deposit due, including interest. For service performed after Sept. 30, 1982, credit is given for deposit service when computing your length of service. If the deposit is not made for that service, that period of service will be removed from your annuity computation.

- **Redeposit Service**—Redeposit Service is service time for which your retirement contributions were refunded. If the refund was based on a separation prior to Oct. 1, 1990, you are not required to pay the redeposit in order to receive credit for the refunded service. Full credit for the refunded service will be allowed in determining annuity eligibility; however, your annuity will be reduced for failure to make the redeposit. If the refund was based on a separation after Sept. 30, 1990, disability retirement, or death-in-service, full credit for the refunded service will be allowed in determining eligibility, but if the redeposit is not made the service is not creditable for computation of your annuity.

To compute your reduced monthly annuity, divide the redeposit amount owed, including interest, by the Present Value Factor for your age at retirement. Subtract this figure from your estimated monthly annuity.

## CSRS Present Value Factors:
### Annuities beginning on or after October 1, 1994

| Age at Retirement | Reduction | Age at Retirement | Reduction | Age at Retirement | Reduction |
|---|---|---|---|---|---|
| 50 | 234.8 | 57 | 202.3 | 64 | 168.2 |
| 51 | 230.2 | 58 | 197.6 | 65 | 163.0 |
| 52 | 225.9 | 59 | 193.1 | 66 | 157.9 |
| 53 | 221.4 | 60 | 188.7 | 67 | 153.1 |
| 54 | 216.8 | 61 | 183.7 | 68 | 148.0 |
| 55 | 211.9 | 62 | 178.3 | 69 | 142.8 |
| 56 | 207.2 | 63 | 173.2 | 70 | 138.0 |

## Can I calculate my annuity?

To estimate your basic annuity, first figure your high-3 average salary and then your creditable service time. After determining these figures, there are several methods you can use to estimate your federal annuity. The following example is for an employee with a high-3 average salary of $46,000, retiring after 32 years of federal service.

## *Approximate Annuity Calculation – An Example\**

| % | x | High-3 Average Salary | x | Years of Service | = | Total |
|---|---|---|---|---|---|---|
| 1.50% | x | $46,000 = 690 | x | 5 | = | $ 3,450 |
| 1.75% | x | $46,000 = 855 | x | 5 | = | $ 4,275 |
| 2.00% | x | $46,000 = 920 | x | 22 | = | $ 20,240 |
| | | Annual Annuity | | | = | $ 27,965 |
| | | Monthly Annuity | | | = | $ 2,330 |

\* Before reductions for survivor benefits, deductions for health benefits, insurance, taxes

When you retire, your official annuity is computed by OPM. Your personnel office can provide you with an annuity estimate. OPM's computation is based on viewing your federal service time in three distinct tiers. Each tier has a different multiplier. Your first five years of service have a multiplier of 1.5 percent. Years six through 10 have a multiplier of 1.75 percent. Any years over 10 years of federal service are multiplied by 2 percent. The figure you multiply in each of these tiers is your high-3 average salary.

One method used to estimate your annuity is the shortcut method. To use this method, complete the following steps:

• Record your high-3 on line 1 of the following work sheet.

• Compute your total service time. Record years, months, and days (line 2).

• Convert unused sick leave into years, months, days and record on line 3\*

• Compute your total service time (lines 2 + 3). Record the total on line 4.

• Multiply your total service time (line 4) by 2. Record this figure on line 6.

• Subtract the number 4 and record the result on line 8. This is the percentage to use in multiplying your high-3 average salary.

• Enter your high-3 salary (line 1) on line 9 and multiply by the percentage from line 8. This is an estimate of your annual annuity. Record the amount on line 11. To figure your estimated monthly annuity, divide this amount by 12.

*\*Sick Leave Chart at the end of this chapter*

## *Basic Annuity Computation Estimate – Shortcut Method*

| | | | | | |
|---|---|---|---|---|---|
| 1. High-3 Average Salary | | | | | $ 46,000 |
| 2. Service | ____yrs. | ____mos. | ____days | | 33 |
| 3. Sick Leave* | ____yrs. | ____ mos. | ____ days | | |
| 4. Total | ____yrs. | ____mos. | | | 33 |
| 5. Multiply by 2 | | | | x 2 | x 2 |
| 6. Total Service (years) | | | | | 66 |
| 7. Subtract 4 from years | | | | - 4 | - 4 |
| 8. Percentage = | | | | | 62% |
| 9. High-3 Average Salary (from Line 1) | | | | | $ 46,000 |
| 10. Multiplied by percent (from Line 8) | | | | | 62% |
| 11. Annual Annuity = | | | | | $ 28,520 |

* See chart at end of chapter

### What benefits will my survivors receive?

As a retiring federal employee you may make choices to provide your survivors with continuing benefits. If you elect these benefits, your annuity will be reduced to partially offset the cost of providing those benefits.

**Employee Death.** The spouse of an employee with 18 months of service who dies before retiring, receives 55 percent of an annuity computed as if the employee had retired on disability retirement as of the date of death. The spouse receives 55 percent of the higher of either (1) or (2):

1. An annuity computed under the CSRS formula based on the deceased employee's high-3 and length of service to date of death, including credit for unused sick leave, or

2. A guaranteed minimum which is the lesser of: 40 percent of the deceased employee's high-3, or annuity obtained after increasing the deceased employee's length of service by the time between the date of death and the date he/she would have been age 60.

Children of an employee receive an annually adjusted amount determined by the number of children. Benefits are set per child. The following rates apply from Dec. 1, 2004, through Nov. 30, 2005. When the child has a living parent who was married to the employee or retiree, the benefit payable is the lesser of:

- $402 per month per child; or
- $1,206 per month divided by the number of eligible children

**Annuitant Death.** At the time of retirement, an employee must elect one of the following three options to establish postretirement survivor benefits:

- **A full survivor benefit**—Base annuity reduced by 2.5 percent on the first $3,600 and 10 percent of the remainder of the base. Survivor receives 55 percent of your base annuity for life unless they remarry prior to age 55. However, if the marriage lasted for at least 30 years, the survivor annuity will not be terminated.

## Estimated Cost to Provide a Full Survivor Annuity

| | | | |
|---|---|---|---|
| 1. | Employee's Annual Annuity | $_____ | $ 28,520.00 |
| 2. | Subtract $3,600.00 | - 3,600 | - 3,600.00 |
| 3. | Result | $_____ | 24,920.00 |
| 4. | Multiply by 10% | x .10 | x .10 |
| 5. | Result | $ | 2,492.00 |
| 6. | Add 2.5% of $3,600.00 ($90.00) | + 90.00 | + 90.00 |
| 7. | Result | $ | 2,582.00 |
| 8. | Enter Annual Annuity from Line 1 | $ | 28,520.00 |
| 9. | Enter amount from Line 7 and subtract | | - 2,582.00 |
| 10. | Reduced Annual Annuity = | $ | 25,938.00 |
| 11. | Divide by 12 = reduced monthly annuity | | 2,161.50 |

To estimate your survivor's annuity, subtract $3,600 (a constant) from your annual annuity. Multiply this figure by 10 percent. Add $90 (2.5 percent of $3,600, also a constant) to this total. Subtract this amount from your annual annuity. This is the annual cost of providing a full survivor annuity of 55 percent for your spouse.

- **A partial survivor benefit**—Employee elects any amount less than his base annuity as the base for the survivor benefit. The base annuity is reduced by 2.5 percent of the first $3,600 and 10 percent of any remainder of the survivor base. The survivor receives 55 percent of the elected survivor base for life unless they remarry prior to age 55. However, if the marriage lasted for at least 30 years, the survivor annuity will not be terminated. This option requires spousal consent.

- **No survivor benefit**—Base annuity not reduced. Survivor receives no benefit. This option requires spousal consent. **If at least a partial survivor benefit is not elected, your spouse will be ineligible to continue FEHB coverage after your death.**

Postretirement death benefits for eligible children are the same as the preretirement death benefits for eligible children.

A survivor's annuity, elected at retirement, can be cancelled if you later divorce or if your spouse dies. If an annuitant's spouse dies, the annuitant may have the reduction eliminated and receive the full annuity retroactive to the first of the month after the spouse's death. Send a letter containing the annuitant's full name, date of birth, Social Security number, civil service retirement claim number (CSA), a copy of the death certificate (and a copy of the divorce decree, if applicable) to:

> Office of Personnel Management
> Employee Service and Records Center
> Boyers, PA 16017

Your annuity may also be reduced for failure to make a deposit or redeposit, if you retire under age 55 for reasons other than disability or under the special provisions for law enforcement officers, firefighters, and air traffic controllers. Other reductions occur when a court order has awarded a survivor annuity to a former spouse. OPM must honor court-ordered benefits in divorces granted after May 6, 1985, that provide a survivor annuity to an ex-spouse.

To qualify:

- the marriage must have lasted at least nine months,

- the employee must have had at least 18 months of federal service, and
- the former spouse must not have remarried prior to age 55.

## What if I am disabled?

To qualify for CSRS disability retirement, you must have at least five years of creditable civilian service. You must be totally disabled for useful and efficient service in the position occupied and for service in any vacant position in the agency at the same grade and pay level and in the same commuting area. The disability must be expected to last at least one year or to terminate in death. A determination of total disability is made by OPM when the information in the file indicates that there is a service deficiency caused by disease or injury of sufficient degree to preclude useful and efficient service. Offset employees must file for Social Security when they file for a disability retirement. If you have less than 22 years of service, your disability is computed at 40 percent of your high-3. If you have 22 years or more of service, your disability is computed as if you retired.

A disability annuitant receives the higher of:

- The amount obtained under the general formula for computing the basic annual annuity (the earned annuity); or
- The guaranteed minimum disability annuity.

The guaranteed minimum disability is the lessor of:

- 40 percent x the high-3 average salary (which provides you with an annuity as if you worked 21 years and 11 months); or
- The amount obtained under the general formula, giving you additional service credit as if you had worked until age 60.

Because of percentage/age limitations, a guaranteed minimum annuity offers no advantage to a retiree if you completed 21 years and 11 months of creditable service, owe no deposit or redeposit for previous civilian service, or are age 60 or older. Contrary to popular opinion, there is no tax advantage with a disability retirement.

## As CSRS can I qualify for Social Security?

The government pension offset reduces or eliminates your ability to receive a spousal Social Security benefit if you're a federal employee. It does not affect your CSRS pension or the Social Security you earned before or after your federal career. It only affects your ability to draw a spouse's Social Security benefit. Two-thirds of your annuity is used to offset, or eliminate, any spousal benefit you might receive.

For example, your spouse works in the private sector and elects to take Social Security at age 65. He or she receives a $700-per-month Social Security benefit. As their spouse, you're entitled, at full retirement age, to one-half of their $700 per month, or $350. As a civil service retiree, however, you are impacted by the offset. Let's assume that your CSRS annuity is $1,000 per month. Two-thirds of your annuity, or $666, would totally offset the $350 you would receive; therefore, you would receive nothing on your spouse's Social Security record. In most cases, the Government Pension Offset eliminates a federal employee's ability to receive benefits from their spouse's Social Security

If you're eligible to receive both a civil service retirement pension and a Social Security benefit, the Social Security benefit will probably be reduced. The windfall elimination provision severely reduces such "windfall" Social Security benefits for retired workers whose primary employment was not covered by Social Security. A different formula is used to compute a federal worker's Social Security benefit, resulting in a lower benefit. There are exceptions to the provision; for further information contact your personnel office or local Social Security office.

Your Social Security benefit is based on your total earnings under Social Security indexed for inflation. When your total indexed earnings have been determined, they are divided by 35 years to determine your Average Indexed Yearly Earnings. That figure is then divided by 12 to give the Average Indexed Monthly Earnings (AIME).

After your AIME is determined, the windfall elimination provision takes effect. In the first tier of a three-tier formula, a CSRS employee's earnings are multiplied by 40 to 90 percent (usually 40 percent rather than the 90 percent used in the private sector). This reduces your benefits. Your benefits are unaffected by computations in the second and third tiers of the formula. Typically, the reduction in your Social Security benefit will be 40 to 50 percent since the Social Security earnings of most CSRS employees occurred early in their careers.

## What is the CSRS Offset Plan?

The CSRS Offset Plan is CSRS modified for employees who are mandatorily covered by Social Security but who chose to remain in CSRS. Employees covered by the Offset Plan are those rehired into the Civil Service on or after Jan. 1, 1984, who had a break in service of one year or more, but who, as of the date of separation, had at least five years of federal civilian service.

If you are in the Offset Plan, you cannot return to the pure CSRS. You have a choice of remaining in the Offset Plan or transferring to FERS. You are allowed six months to make the transfer decision. Employees in the Offset Plan must pay the Social Security tax, plus a small contribution (0.8 percent) to the CSRS fund.

Since Offset Plan employees are basically CSRS employees, they receive a CSRS annuity until age 62, at which time they may become eligible for Social Security. If you are ineligible for Social Security at age 62, you will continue to receive your full CSRS benefit. If you are eligible for Social Security at age 62, then your CSRS annuity is reduced to "offset" that part of your Social Security coverage, which is subject to the Offset Plan.

The CSRS benefit is reduced by a set formula:

(Social Security Benefit) x (Years of Offset Service) ÷ 40

For example, an employee retiring at age 60 with 30 years of service and a high-3 of $40,000 has an annuity of $22,500 (using the general formula—56.25 percent of $40,000). Assume he had 10 years of CSRS service—20 years as a CSRS Offset employee and 10 years in private industry. Now assume that his Social Security benefit is $10,000, $7,000 from the years under the Offset Plan and $3,000 from the years in private industry.

(Social Security Benefit) x (Years of Offset Service) ÷ 40

$10,000 x 20 = $200,000

$200,000 ÷ 40 = $5,000

When you do this computation, keep in mind that your Social Security benefit is subject to the windfall elimination provision if you have less than 30 years of service. The $22,500 annuity will be reduced by $5,000 to $17,500. The retiree is eligible for a full Social Security benefit of $10,000 (based on years in private industry and the Offset Plan); therefore, the benefit will be $27,500 ($17,500 + $10,000). If you had only CSRS time and 10 years of private Social Security, your benefit at age 62 would be $22,500 plus $3,000 from Social Security for a total of $25,500. Because of the Offset Plan, this employee would be slightly—$2,000—better off than a pure CSRS employee.

## What are Voluntary Contribution Accounts?

All CSRS employees who do not owe a deposit or redeposit are eligible to participate in Voluntary Contribution Accounts. The option is open only to CSRS employees. Before contributing, you must first complete any deposit for service not covered by retirement deductions, or repay any outstanding refunds.

**Contributions.** Eligible employees make voluntary contributions to the Civil Service Retirement and Disability Fund to purchase additional annuity. Contributions are limited to 10 percent of your total lifetime pay and are sent, by check or money order, directly to OPM in multiples of $25. At retirement, each $100 of contributions may be used to purchase additional annuity at the rate of $7 per year, plus 20 cents for each full year an employee is over age 55.

**Fund Options.** The Voluntary Contribution Account has only one investment fund—the Civil Service Retirement and Disability Fund. The variable interest rate is determined by the Treasury Department at the beginning of each year.

**Tax Status.** Unlike contributions to the Thrift Savings Plan, these contributions are not tax deferred, but the earnings are tax deferred until withdrawal. CSRS employees may contribute to both plans. However, financial planners recommend that you invest the maximum in the fully tax deferred TSP before making voluntary contributions.

**Withdrawal Options.** You can withdraw all voluntary contributions, with interest, at any time before you receive additional annuity based on those contributions. You are allowed only one withdrawal. Once the money is withdrawn, you cannot reopen the account.

**Application Process.** OPM administers the voluntary contributions program. Employees wishing to participate should complete an application (SF 2804), and submit it to the Office of Personnel, AHME, Room W-3058, Washington, D.C. 20537. OPM will explain how to make contributions when your application is approved.

## FERS

If you were hired after Jan. 1, 1984, you are under the Federal Employees Retirement System. It is a very different retirement system than is CSRS. FERS was designed to acknowledge that today's federal workforce is more transient—so Social Security is a key component. If you change careers, your Social Security travels with you. This portability is important in a workforce where the average 40-year-old has already had eight different jobs.

The second feature of FERS, the Thrift Savings Plan, shifts much of the responsibility for a financially secure future from the government's shoulders to yours. Since 1987, federal employees have had the opportunity to participate in the Thrift Savings Plan. If you are under FERS, you can contribute up to 15 percent of your salary and the federal government will match 5 percent of that contribution dollar for dollar. The money you have withheld is all tax deferred. Over time this can add up to a very sizable nest egg. From the government's standpoint, the Thrift Plan means your financial future is now more of a planning partnership. If you don't do your part in funding your TSP account, your future may be less secure.

The last component of FERS is the Basic Benefit Plan or pension. It is smaller than the CSRS pension because FERS employees also have Social Security and more liberal TSP options.

The Federal Employees Retirement System was first available to employees in the Open Season of 1987 when some CSRS employees transferred into FERS. All federal employee first hired after January 1984 are automatically FERS employees. FERS covers:

• Anyone first hired or rehired (with a break in service of one year or more and less than five years of civilian service) after Dec. 31, 1983;

- Employees rehired from Jan. 1, 1984, through Dec. 31, 1986, who had less than five years of civilian service on Dec. 31, 1986; and

- Employees who elected to transfer from CSRS.

If you retire under FERS, you have three sources of retirement funds: Social Security, a FERS annuity, and your Thrift Savings Plan account.

**Social Security.** Like employees in the private sector, you contribute 7.65 percent of your salary to the Social Security system. Of your contribution, 6.2 percent is a Social Security tax and 1.45 percent is for Medicare. When you become eligible for Social Security, contributions from the current workforce will provide your benefit. If you leave federal service before retirement your Social Security travels with you to your new employer.

**The Basic Benefit Plan.** FERS regular employees contribute 0.8 percent of their salary to the Basic Benefit Plan or FERS Basic Annuity, administered by OPM.

**The Thrift Savings Plan.** The final source of FERS retirement funds is the Thrift Savings Plan, which is administered by the Thrift Investment Board. A FERS employee may contribute up to 15 percent of salary in 2005, with a 5 percent government match, to any of the investment choices available in the Thrift Savings Plan. In 2006 and beyond, the contribution limit will be a dollar amount established annually by the Internal Revenue Service (IRS).

### When am I eligible?

If you have five or more years of creditable service under CSRS or FERS or a combination of both, you are vested and have a right to receive benefits from one of the retirement systems. Your benefit is an annuity when age and service requirements are met. To receive disability or to provide a survivor benefit you need 18 months of service.

Many employees choose not to take a deferred annuity and, instead, withdraw all the money they've contributed when they leave federal service. With even moderate inflation, taking a deferred annuity means that those dollars won't buy as much at age 62 as they might today. Think carefully about whether to leave the money in or take it out. If you choose to withdraw all of your contributions at the time of separation, the money will be paid to you with a market rate of interest. However, if you are subsequently reemployed under FERS, you will not be able to use the previous FERS employment for retirement purposes. **Refunds under FERS permanently extinguish service credit.** As a general rule, it's usually wisest to leave the money in the system, taking it as a deferred annuity. This is because you pay very little compared to the benefits you will receive— only about 5 percent of the total value of your Basic Benefits.

## What service counts toward retirement?

The largest part of FERS creditable service, for most people, is all time between the date they were hired and the date of separation. Any employee who began a federal career after January 1984 is automatically covered by FERS. Any CSRS employee who transferred to FERS between July and December 1987 has been covered by FERS since the date of their transfer. If you transferred with at least five years of vested CSRS service, part of your annuity will be computed under CSRS and part will be computed under FERS. If you transferred with less than five years of service, all of your time is considered to be FERS service. A federal employee subject to the CSRS interim provisions during 1984-86 paid 1.3 percent CSRS salary deductions and full Social Security deductions. This service can also be counted as FERS creditable service for an employee who transferred to FERS.

As a general rule, any *active military service* that ended with an honorable discharge can be credited toward your FERS retirement. If your military service took place before 1957, you are given gratuitous credit. If it occurred after 1956, you must pay 3 percent of your total base military pay, plus interest, for that service to be credited toward your retirement. Your military time is then added to your total FERS service and significantly increases your annuity payout.

Interest charges will not be added to what you owe for military service if you make the deposit within the three-year interest-free period. Interest starts and is compounded annually beginning two years from the date first employed. The earliest possible interest posting for an unpaid military service deposit is Jan. 1, 1990. The interest rate has been variable (money market rates) since 1985. No credit is allowed for any period of retired military service unless the retiree waives receipt of military retired pay. The retiree does not have to waive retired pay awarded based on a service-connected disability, incurred in combat, or based on age and service in the reserves.

Sick leave earned while a FERS employee cannot be used for retirement eligibility or in computing your annuity. Sick leave earned by a FERS employee, when previously covered by CSRS, can be added to the CSRS component for annuity computation at the time of retirement. To have a CSRS component, you must have elected to transfer to FERS and had at least five years of creditable civilian service at the time of transfer. You'll receive credit for the lesser amount of sick leave you had either at the time you transferred to FERS or at the time of retirement.

- **Other Creditable Service**—Credit is generally given for both civilian and military service performed for the federal government.

- **Leave Without Pay (LWOP)**—Other creditable service can include periods of leave without pay. Credit is given for up to six months per calendar year.

- **Part-Time Employment**—For eligibility, full credit is granted for all time between the date of hire and the date of separation for part-time service. The annuity is computed by determining the percentage of time you worked over your entire federal career times the high-3 that you would have earned if you had been full-time.

- **Deposit Service**—Any period of civilian service not covered by FERS is called deposit or non-deduction service. To be creditable for both retirement eligibility and annuity computation, the non-deduction service must have been performed prior to Jan. 1, 1989, and a deposit must be made. A deposit may not be made for non-deduction service performed on or after Jan. 1, 1989. Such service is not creditable for eligibility or computation. Non-deduction service includes service now credited under FERS for which deductions were made under CSRS and were refunded before you first became covered under FERS. The deposit due is 1.3 percent of your base pay earned during the period of non-deduction service, plus interest. FERS service for which retirement contributions were refunded is not creditable for retirement eligibility or annuity computation.

## How much will my annuity be?

The FERS Basic Benefit Plan provides retirement benefits based on years of service, age, and your average high-3. An employee with enough years of service can retire at the minimum retirement age and receive unreduced benefits.

An employee can retire at age 62 with five or more years of service, at age 60 with 20 or more years of service, or at the Minimum Retirement Age with 30 or more years of service. Computing your FERS annuity is relatively easy. The amount you receive when you leave federal service, or retire, is a combination of your Social Security, your Basic Annuity, and your contributions to the Thrift Plan.

## *FERS Minimum Retirement Age (MRA)*

| Year of Birth | MRA | Year of Birth | MRA |
|---|---|---|---|
| Before 1948 | 55 | 1965 | 56 & 2 mo. |
| 1948 | 55 & 2 mo. | 1966 | 56 & 4 mo. |
| 1949 | 55 & 4 mo. | 1967 | 56 & 6 mo. |
| 1950 | 55 & 6 mo. | 1968 | 56 & 8 mo. |
| 1951 | 55 & 8 mo. | 1969 | 56 & 10 mo. |
| 1952 | 55 & 10 mo. | 1970+ | 57 |
| 1953-64 | 56 | | |

| Retirement | Age | Years of Service |
|---|---|---|
| Optional/Voluntary | MRA | 30 |
| | 60 | 20 |
| | 62 | 5 |
| | MRA | +10* |

*Your annuity will be reduced 5% for each year you are under age 62. Deferred Annuity payable at age 62 with 5 years of service

| Retirement | Age | Years of Service |
|---|---|---|
| Involuntary/Early Optional | 50 | 20 |
| (Discontinued Service) | Any age | 25 |
| Deferred | 62 | 5 |
| | 60 | 20 |
| | MRA | 30 |
| | MRA | +10 |
| Disability | Any Age | 18 months |

Depending on your age and your years of service at retirement, different computation formulas apply. If you retire before age 62, the following computation formula is used:

1% x average high-3 x Years & Months of Service

If you retire at age 62 or later, with less than 20 years of service, the computation formula is:

1% x average high-3 x Years & Months of Service

If you retire at age 62 or later, with 20 or more years of service, use the following formula:

1.1% x average high-3 x Years & Months of Service

For a 57-year-old employee with 30 years of service and a high-3 average salary of $60,000, the calculation is:

1% x $60,000 x 30 years

$600 x 30 = $18,000

If you elect to receive the monthly benefit at the Minimum Retirement Age, and if you have at least 10 but less than 30 years of service, the benefit will be permanently reduced 5 percent a year for each year you are under 62.

If you leave federal service before retirement, you can withdraw your retirement contributions. If you do, you forfeit the ability to receive credit for that period of service under FERS should you later return to federal employment.

## What is a deferred annuity?

If you leave federal employment after five years of creditable service for any reason other than death, disability, or retirement, and you do not withdraw your contributions from FERS, you will be eligible to receive *deferred benefits* from the FERS Basic Benefit Plan. If you have creditable service of at least 20 years but less that 30 years at the time that you leave federal service, you are eligible for the deferred benefit at age 60 without a reduction in your annuity. If you have 30 years or more of creditable service when you leave, you are eligible for the deferred benefit upon reaching your MRA without any reduction in your annuity. You are also eligible to received the deferred benefit (with a reduction prior to age 62) at any time after you meet your MRA with at least 10 years of creditable service. The reduction will be 5 percent of your basic annuity for each year you are under age 62.

## Can I retire early?

You can retire with fewer years of service and receive reduced retirement benefits if you have reached your MRA and completed at least 10 years of service, including five years of civilian service. If, as a FERS employee, you do retire early, your annuity is permanently reduced 5 percent for every year you are below age 62. You can defer receipt of your annuity until age 62, however, and reduce or eliminate the 5 percent per year reduction.

## What happens if I am disabled?

To qualify for disability under FERS, you must be totally disabled for useful and efficient service in the position you currently occupy and for service in any vacant position in the agency at the same grade and pay level and in the same commuting area. The determination of total disability is made by OPM when information in the file indicates that there is a service deficiency caused by disease or injury of sufficient degree to preclude useful and efficient service. The disability must be expected to last at least one year or terminate in death. There is no age requirement to apply for a FERS disability retirement, but you must have at least 18 months of creditable civilian service and you must file for Social Security disability.

**Disability Computation.** An employee under age 62 is entitled to:

- First Year: 60 percent of high-3 average salary minus 100 percent of any Social Security benefits payable.

- Second and Subsequent Years until age 62: 40 percent of high-3 minus 60 percent of any Social Security benefits payable.

The month the retiree reaches age 62, the disability annuity is recomputed using the basic annuity formula (1 percent if less than 20 years of service or 1.1 percent if 20 or more years times the high-3). The retiree receives additional service credit for the total time on the disability retirement rolls. The high-3 average salary is increased by all FERS COLAs the retiree received during retirement.

When an employee age 62 or older applies for disability retirement, they receive their earned annuity based on total years of creditable service and high-3 average salary. **No COLAs are provided during the first year on the disability rolls if receiving 60 percent of the high-3.**

### What will my survivors receive?

**Employee Death.** The spouse of an employee with at least 18 months of creditable civilian service but less than 10 years of total service who dies after Dec. 1, 2004, and before Dec. 1, 2005, receives a payment of $25,527.58, indexed each year for inflation. This payment can be taken as a lump sum or in 36 monthly installments. They also receive the larger of either:

- 50 percent of your final annual salary at the time of death; or

- 50 percent of your high-3.

The surviving spouse is also potentially eligible for the deceased employees' Social Security benefits and TSP death benefits. The spouse of a deceased employee with 10 years or more of service will receive the above benefits, plus an annuity equal to 50 percent of the employee's accrued basic benefit. The employee's children receive an amount that varies depending upon the number of children. Benefits are reduced by any Social Security benefits that are received. The following rates for children's benefits apply from Dec. 1, 2004, through Nov. 30, 2005. When the child has a living parent who was married to the employee or retiree, the benefit payable is the lesser of:

• $402 per month per child; or

• $1,206 per month divided by the number of eligible children

**Annuitant Death.** At the time of retirement, an employee must elect one of the following options to establish postretirement survivor benefits:

• **Full survivor benefit**—Base annuity reduced by 10 percent. Your survivor receives 50 percent of your base annuity for life unless they remarry prior to age 55. However, if the marriage lasted for at least 30 years, the survivor annuity will not be terminated.

• **One-half survivor benefit**—Base annuity reduced by 5 percent. Survivor receives 25 percent of your base annuity for life unless they remarry prior to age 55. However, if the marriage lasted for at least 30 years, the survivor annuity will not be terminated.

• **No survivor benefit**—Base annuity not reduced. Survivor receives no benefit.

Elections other than a full benefit require spousal consent. **If at least a partial survivor benefit is not elected, your spouse will be ineligible to continue FEHB coverage after your death.** Postretirement death and preretirement death benefits for eligible children are the same.

## What is the Special Annuity Supplement?

The Special Annuity Supplement is a bridge payment to be paid from the time you retire until age 62. At age 62 the payment stops, and Social Security begins. The supplement is subject to the same earnings test as is used with Social Security benefits. It is paid to employees who retire with an immediate benefit at the MRA after at least 30 years of service; at age 60 after at least 20 years of service; and on retirement under the special provisions relating to law enforcement, firefighters, and air-traffic controllers.

The supplement is calculated by first estimating your full career (40 years) Social Security benefit. It then approximates the amount of that benefit that was earned while working under FERS. The formula is:

(Estimated Social Security Benefit) x (Years of FERS Civilian Service) ÷ 40

If you decide to retire at age 60 and your full career Social Security benefit at age 62 is equal to $12,000 a year, and you worked in service covered under FERS for 20 years, the proportion earned under FERS is equal to 20 years divided by 40 (full career) or .50. The supplement would be calculated as follows:

Estimated Social Security Benefit x Years of Service ÷ 40 = FERS Supplement

$12,000 x 20 ÷ 40 = $6,000

$12,000 x .50 = $6,000

Therefore, you would receive, in addition to the FERS basic annuity, a Special Retirement Supplement of $6,000 per year. The supplement is available only if you retire before age 62 and is only paid until you reach age 62.

## The Earnings Test

If you retire under FERS before age 62, but you are employed elsewhere after retirement, you may lose all or part of the supplement. The reduction depends on your level of earnings after retirement. The reduction applies to the supplement only, not the basic benefit. A retiree can have a minimum level of earnings without losing any of the supplement. If the earnings are above the minimum level, however, the supplement will be reduced. OPM will ask you for a statement of earnings each year you are eligible to receive the supplement.

# COLAs

Both CSRS and FERS retirees receive cost-of-living adjustments (COLAs). The amount of the COLA is determined by comparing the Consumer Price Index for Wage Earners and Clerical Workers (CPI-W) for the third calendar quarter of the current year with the same calendar quarter of the preceding year. Under CSRS the resulting percentage will be applied to the retiree or survivor annuity effective December 1 and payable in the January check.

CSRS retirees and survivors will receive a full COLA. FERS retirees do not receive a COLA until they are age 62 unless they retire on FERS disability. Disability retirees receive a COLA after one year on the disability roles. The FERS COLA is generally referred to as a COLA minus one. Actually, if the percentage is greater than 3 percent, it is a COLA minus one; if it is between 2 percent and 3 percent, the COLA will be 2 percent; if it is less than 2 percent, the full COLA will be paid.

Initial COLAs are prorated, depending upon the number of months the recipient has been retired. For example, an employee retiring during the first three days of December 2005 would receive the full COLA that becomes effective in December 2005. One retiring in January would receive 11/12 of the COLA given on Jan. 1, 2006.

## The Lump Sum

At retirement all retirees receive a lump sum payment for all remaining annual leave accrued during the current leave year. You will also receive a lump sum payment for annual leave carried over from previous years. The lump sum payment is calculated by multiplying the number of hours of leave by your hourly rate of pay, plus other types of pay you would have received while on annual leave, excluding any allowances that are paid for the sole purpose of retaining a federal employee in government service. Locality pay or other similar geographic adjustments and across-the-board annual adjustments are included in the lump sum payment.

## The Simplified General Rule

The Simplified General Rule determines the federal income tax liability on your annuity. The recovery factors (number of anticipated payments) were increased for annuities starting after Nov. 18, 1996. The Simplified General Rule became mandatory after this date. To determine the tax-free portion of your annuity you need to know the amount you contributed to the retirement fund and the number of monthly payments. OPM will tell you the amount of your contributions. The number of monthly payments is determined by the IRS.

The following table is used if you do not elect any survivor benefits.

| Age at Annuity Start Date | Number of Payments |
|---|---|
| 55 and under | 360 |
| 56-60 | 310 |
| 61-65 | 260 |
| 66-70 | 210 |
| 71 and over | 160 |

Divide your total contributions by the number of payments. For example, Bob's annuity start date was Oct. 1, 2005. He was age 55 and his total contributions were $42,150. To figure the tax-free portion of his annuity, divide $42,150 by 360. This amount, $117.08, of his gross monthly annuity is tax free. This amount remains the same until he recovers the amount he contributed. IRS *Publication 721* describes using this formula when computing your taxes.

*The Taxpayer Relief Act of 1997* created a new table for figuring the tax-free amount if a survivor annuity is provided. The table is based on the combined ages of the annuitant and the person for whom the survivor annuity is being provided. This provision was effective with annuities beginning after Dec. 31, 1997. Use the following table if you have elected a survivor benefit.

| Combined Age of Annuitants | Number of Payments |
|---|---|
| Not more than 110 | 410 |
| 111-120 | 360 |
| 121-130 | 310 |
| 131-140 | 260 |
| 141 and over | 210 |

## Health Benefits (FEHB)

Your eligibility to continue group health benefits is an important factor to consider when planning retirement. The Federal Employees Health Benefits program is a voluntary contributory program, open to almost all employees. The federal government contributes to the cost of the plans with employees paying their share through payroll deductions.

Employees are offered various group plans, which reduce the cost of health care services, including coverage for prolonged illness or serious accidents. You can enroll in the plan of your choice. If you elect to enroll but later wish to change enrollment, you may do so only during the annual open season. If you elect not to enroll when eligible for coverage, you must wait for an event—e.g., changes in marital/family status or relocating from an area served by an HMO—to enroll or make an enrollment change.

## Premium Conversion

In October 2000, OPM implemented FEHB premium conversion for most federal employees in the Executive Branch. Employees who participate in premium conversion will have their salary reduced and the amount of that reduction applied toward the FEHB premium. Since the participating employee will not receive the amount of the salary reduction, it will not be considered gross income for federal tax, Social Security and Medicare taxes. State and local income tax is also reduced for most employees, except for the state of New Jersey and the Commonwealth of Puerto Rico.

Premium conversion will have no effect on deductions for CSRS, FERS, FEGLI, and the TSP. There are disadvantages to premium conversion. Employees will not be able to deduct FEHB premiums as a medical deduction on their income tax and must wait for an FEHB open season or qualifying life event to cancel coverage or change from a self-and-family to self-only enrollment. Paying premiums with pretax money reduces your reported earnings and may result in a lower Social Security benefit.

## Continuing FEHB

Your FEHB can continue into retirement provided the following requirements are met:

1. You retire on an immediate annuity, and
2. You have been enrolled or covered as a family member in a plan covered by the health benefits program for five years of service immediately preceding your retirement, or for all service since your first enrollment opportunity. The time you are covered under the *Uniformed*

*Service Health Benefits Program* (TRICARE) is considered a federal plan for continuous coverage if you are covered under an FEHB enrollment at the time of your retirement.

There is an automatic waiver of the minimum enrollment of five years for certain employees retiring with buyouts or taking early optional retirement. For inquiries, call this special OPM number: 202-606-0191. As a retiree, you're entitled to the same benefits and government contributions as any active employee in the same health plan. Your costs will be the same as those of active employees and are usually deducted from your annuity. Your agency will automatically transfer the enrollment to OPM. You don't need to do anything unless you want to make changes in the coverage.

## Temporary Continuation of Coverage

If you leave federal service before you retire, or are ineligible to carry the coverage into retirement, you are eligible to enroll in the Temporary Continuation of Coverage program (TCC). This program allows a separated employee to continue coverage under FEHB without a break for up to 18 months from the date of his/her separation. You will be responsible for paying both your share and the government share of the premium plus an administrative fee of approximately 2 percent of the premium. You are allowed 60 days from the date of separation in which to make this decision.

# Life Insurance (FEGLI)

The Federal Employees Group Life Insurance (FEGLI) program offers two kinds of term life insurance, providing benefits upon the death of the insured—Basic Life Insurance and Optional Life Insurance.

## Basic Life Insurance

The Basic option provides an amount of coverage based on your annual basic salary, which includes locality pay. All eligible employees are automatically covered for basic life insurance under the FEGLI program, unless it is specifically waived.

• Equal to annual basic pay (rounded to next $1,000, plus $2,000).

- Double life insurance benefits until age 36, decreasing at 10 percent per year until age 45 at which time extra coverage will end.

- Accidental death and dismemberment coverage while active employee, no accidental death and dismemberment coverage in retirement.

## Optional Life Insurance

Additional optional insurance may be elected within 31 days of being permanently hired. Basic Life must have been elected to be eligible for Optional Life.

- **Option A:** Standard-Additional $10,000 life insurance coverage, additional $10,000 accidental death and dismemberment coverage until retirement.

- **Option B:** Additional-Additional life insurance coverage equal to one, two, three, four, or five times actual rate of basic pay (rounded to next $1,000).

- **Option C:** Family-Additional life insurance coverage equal to one, two, three, four, or five times $5,000 on your spouse and $2,500 on eligible children.

If you do not want Basic Life and/or Optional Life insurance, you can decline it by submitting the proper form to the Personnel Office. If, at a later date, you decide on insurance coverage, you can request it if you meet the following requirements:

- At least one year must have elapsed between the effective date of your last waiver (or declination) and the date of the request for insurance.

- You must furnish, at your expense, adequate medical evidence of insurability.

If you leave federal employment before you retire or have completed 12 months in a non-pay status, you have 31 days to convert to an individual, non-group policy. Life insurance coverage can be continued into retirement provided certain requirements are met.

| Insurance $ at retirement | At age 65 & retired | |
|---|---|---|
| **Basic**<br>75% Reduction | $.3250/$1,000 of BIA* | No cost. Starts to reduce 2% per month; reduces down to 25% of amount at retirement |
| **Basic**<br>50% Reduction | $.9250 per $1,000 | Cost is $.60 per $1,000 of BIA. Starts to reduce 1% per month; reduces to 50% of amount at retirement |
| **Basic**<br>No Reduction | $2.1550 per $1,000 | Cost is $1.83 per $1,000 of BIA. No reduction in coverage |
| **Standard**<br>Option A | Premiums based on age band** | No cost. Coverage reduces 2% per month until it reaches 25% of preretirement amount. ($2,500) |
| **Additional**<br>Option B | Premiums based on age band** | Full Reduction. No Cost. Coverage starts to reduce 2% per month until coverage ends.<br><br>No Reduction-Premiums continue to be withheld from annuity based on age band. |
| **Family**<br>Option C | Premiums based on age band** and number of multiples | Full Reduction-No cost. Coverage reduces 2% per month until coverage ends.<br><br>No Reduction-Premiums continue to be withheld based on age band. |

* Basic Insurance Amount is your final annual basic pay, rounded to the next exact $1,000, plus $2,000. Your BIA reduces after you are retired and are age 65, unless you have elected No Reduction

** Consult OPM or your agency for the age bands.

## Age Bands: Monthly Withholding Costs

| Age Group | Option A-Standard | Option B-Additional | Option C-Family |
|---|---|---|---|
| Under age 35 | $ 0.65 | $0.065 | $ 0.59 |
| 35-39 | $ 0.87 | $0.087 | $ 0.74 |
| 40-44 | $ 1.30 | $0.130 | $ 1.00 |
| 45-49 | $ 1.95 | $0.195 | $ 1.30 |
| 50-54 | $ 3.03 | $0.303 | $ 1.95 |
| 55-59 | $ 5.85 | $0.607 | $ 3.14 |
| 60-64 | $13.00 | $1.300 | $ 5.63 |
| 65-69 | —— | $1.56 | $ 6.50 |
| 70-74 | —— | $2.60 | $ 7.37 |
| 75-79 | —— | $3.90 | $ 9.75 |
| 80+ | —— | $5.20 | $13.00 |

**Designating Beneficiaries.** You do not need to name a beneficiary if you wish to have death benefits paid in the following order of precedence:

1. Your widow or widower.

2. Your child or children in equal shares, with the share of any deceased child distributed among the descendants of that child.

3. Your parents in equal shares or the entire amount to the surviving parent.

4. The duly appointed executor or administrator of your estate.

5. Your next of kin under the laws of your domicile at the time of your death.

If you do wish to name a beneficiary, and you are survived by a designated beneficiary, the benefits will be paid to the beneficiary. To name a beneficiary or change a prior designation, complete a new designation. The designation must be as follows:

1. Signed by you.

2. Witnessed by two persons, neither of whom is a beneficiary (a witness to the designation may not receive payment as a beneficiary).

3. Received by your employing office (for employees) or retirement system (for annuitants) before your death.

Death benefits, in the event of an employee death, are paid from four sources:

1. Federal Employees Group Life Insurance (FEGLI).

2. Civil Service Retirement System or Federal Employees Retirement System.

3. Unpaid Compensation (Unused Annual Leave and Unpaid Salary).

4. Thrift Savings Plan.

If you do wish to name a beneficiary other than those listed, or if you do not wish to follow the order of precedence, complete a designation-of-beneficiary form for the type of fund for which you wish to designate. You may request the following designations-of-beneficiary forms from your servicing Personnel Office: *SF 2823 for FEGLI, SF 2808 for CSRS, SF 3102 for FERS, SF 1152 for Unpaid Compensation of a Deceased Civilian Employee,* and *Form TSP-3 for the Thrift Savings Plan.* It is important that designations be kept current in order that death benefits are paid in accordance with your wishes.

## Long-Term-Care Insurance

This insurance became available in 2002. There are currently no open seasons scheduled, but you may still make an application. If you have aging parents or are concerned about your own long-term-care needs the government program is worth exploring. Information and application forms are available through the website, *www.ltcfeds.com,* or by calling 1-800-582-3337.

### Who is eligible?

Federal employees, retirees, survivor annuitants, adult children, spouses, and parents of employees are eligible participants. Newly hired employees and members of the uniformed services and their spouses are subject to the short form of underwriting consisting of several general health questions. Current employees and retirees are subject to the long form of underwriting.

The program is offered by *Long Term Care Partners*, a partnership of *John Hancock Life Insurance Company and Metropolitan Life Insurance Company.* The premium amount is determined by the enrollee's age at the time LTC Partners receives your application and the plan you choose. OPM has posted a list of Frequently Asked Questions(FAQ) about the new insurance on their website, opm.gov. The insurance has four basic options.

| *Available Plans* | *Monthly Premiums:* | |
| --- | --- | --- |
| | *45-year-old* | *60-year-old* |
| **Facilities 100** 3 years of coverage at $100/day | $11.00 | $27.80 |
| **Comprehensive 100** 3 years of coverage at $150/day | $16.40 | $40.60 |
| **Comprehensive 150** 5 years of coverage at $150/day | $28.50 | $72.30 |
| **Comprehensive 150+** 5 yrs of coverage at $150/day with unlimited coverage | $37.20 | $94.20 |

The waiting period before benefits could begin is 90 days on all three plans. Benefit amounts can be customized in $25 increments (from $50 a day to a maximum $300). Enrollees can select 5 percent automatic inflation protection or elect to have benefits remain the same but have the opportunity to purchase additional coverage, at higher prices, every two years. Premiums will be based on age, and the cost for employees recently retired and those eligible for retirement will be higher.

Premiums will also be affected by which benefits are chosen, the length of the policy, the waiting period, and the inflation protection selected. Employees and retirees will pay the entire premium. There will be no employer contribution. The coverage is guaranteed renewable and is also portable at the same premium.

## What are the benefits?

Enrollees select a maximum benefit and policy length. The maximum weekly benefit can range from $400 to $2,000. Policy length can be three or five years or lifetime. The choices you make in benefits and policy length will determine your "pool of money." The LTC insurance will pay benefits until your "pool of money" is exhausted. The lifetime choice has an inexhaustible "pool of money."

You will be eligible to receive benefits when you meet one of the following two conditions and you satisfy the waiting period you selected.

- You cannot perform two of six activities of daily living and your doctor certifies that the condition is expected to last at least 90 days,

  or

- You have severe cognitive impairment.

# Flexible Spending Accounts

Recently the federal government introduced Flexible Spending Accounts (FSA) for health care. Here's how they work. At the beginning of each year, you elect to defer monies into a savings account. The maximum limit in 2005 is $4,000. When you incur an eligible expense, you simply complete a claim form and submit it (with receipts) for reimbursement from your FSA. You are using pretax dollars to pay for items that are typically not covered by your insurance:

- Medical and dental visits not covered by insurance
- Co-payments
- Deductibles
- Eyeglasses

The most compelling reason to set up an FSA is that by using pretax dollars, you spend less and have more of what you earn to spend on what you want or need.

The down side of FSAs is that it is a "use it or lose it" proposition. If you have any money left in the account after all claims have been paid for the year, you forfeit it. This means you need to use caution in determining how much you will contribute each year. If you find that by mid-November there is a lot of money still in your FSA, you are apt to make purchases that you would not normally make. A second set of prescription sunglasses or an extra chiropractic adjustment is not the best use of your funds. The plan works if you plan carefully and spend down all of the funds each year.

In addition to a medical savings account, you can set up a dependent care FSA for expenses you incur for the care of children under age 13 and dependent adults. The maximum allotment for 2005 was $5,000 if you are married and filing a joint tax return or $2,500 if you file an individual tax return.

## The Thrift Savings Plan

All federal employees are eligible to participate in the Thrift Savings Plan. FERS employees and CSRS employees who transferred to FERS are automatically in the TSP but CSRS employees must elect to participate.

The Thrift Plan is like a 401k plan and has two major tax advantages. First, your contributions reduce your gross income for federal, and in most cases, state income tax purposes. Second, you do not pay current federal income taxes on the earnings on the TSP account until you withdraw the funds. You can continue to defer taxes after leaving federal employment if you transfer the money into an IRA or other qualified plan. If you have at least five years of service, and $3,500 in your account, you can defer withdrawals and leave the account open with the Thrift Investment Board. You can also leave money in the TSP if you're subject to a RIF even if you have less than five years of service. These funds are tax deferred not tax free. When you begin taking distributions you may be in a lower tax bracket. Even if your TSP account is taxed as income, which can usually be minimized, compounding for 20 or more years is well worth the possible tax impact later.

The new record-keeping system for the Thrift Savings Plan means your account is valued on a daily, rather than a monthly, basis. This allows you to transfer money among the available funds as often as once a day. In addition, account balances are being converted to shares—initially valued at $10 each—for all funds.

Beginning in 2006, TSP contributions will be based on IRS limits instead of percentage of employee wage. In 2006 the IRS limit is $15,000 ($20,000 for those over age 50). Increases for 2007 and beyond will be indexed. **Note: Make sure your FERS contributions are spread over the full calendar year. Agency matching contributions are based on the first 5 percent of your contributions withheld each pay period. If you reach the IRS limit on Sept. 30 you would lose the agency matching contributions for October through December.**

FERS employees may contribute up to 15 percent of their salary in 2005. For CSRS employees, contributions to the Thrift Savings Plan are limited to 10 percent of basic pay in 2005. They do not receive an employer matching contribution or an agency automatic contribution. The contribution rate is increasing 1 percent per year until 2006. In 2006 the contribution limits will be the same as those governing 401ks; i.e., the amount you can contribute will be a dollar amount instead of a percentage. The limit will be set by the IRS and be the same as the limit for 401k contributions.

Your contribution is deducted from your pay before federal income tax is computed. Thus, money put into the Thrift Savings Plan is not included on the year end W-2 form. This means that your taxable earnings are lower and you pay less in income tax. This does not affect your gross earnings as a basis for calculating retirement, leave, or Social Security taxes.

The TSP accepts rollovers from 401k plans and conduit IRAs. Participants will deal directly with the TSP Service Office. You still cannot roll over money from a regular IRA, a mutual fund, or savings account. Rollover forms are available on the TSP website or from the TSP Service Office.

Since August 2003, the Thrift Savings Plan has allowed employees age 50 and over to make additional contributions to the TSP under the new **catch-up** provision. The new legislation allows employees who contribute the maximum to their TSP accounts to contribute another $5,000 in 2006 through payroll deductions. Thus, an employee over 50 could contribute $20,000, rather than $15,000, in 2006. The catch-up contribution is not matched by the federal government and follows the allocation already in force in your TSP account.

Because the limits for contributions to the Thrift Savings Plan change each year you will have to complete a Form TSP-1-C each year to elect to make the catch-up contributions.

The Thrift Savings Plan currently offers five investment fund options. The funds differ in risk and potential return:

**Fund I: International Stock Index Investment Fund**—invested in Barclay's EAFE Index Fund, which tracks the Europe, Australasia, and Far East (EAFE) stock index. In a global economy some markets grow at faster rates. This fund allows investors to tap into fast-growing foreign markets. These markets are subject to currency and interest rate fluctuations. This means greater instability. The I Fund will, therefore, be riskier than the C, F, and G funds, but it will also offer the potential for greater reward.

**Fund S: Small Capitalization Stock Investment Fund**—the small cap fund consists of stock of small companies with growth potential. Like the I fund, the S Fund will carry greater risk since small company stock can be quite volatile. It is invested in Barclay's Extended Market Index Fund, which tracks the Wilshire 4500 stock index.

**Fund C: Common Stock Index Investment Fund**—invested in Barclay's Equity Index Fund, which tracks the Standard and Poor's 500 Stock Index. The index includes 500 stocks, representing 84 separate industries. All are U.S. stocks, and most are traded on the New York Stock Exchange. This fund provides the opportunity to earn greater returns, but it also involves more risk. Investment earnings will fluctuate, according to market conditions, and the principal amount is not guaranteed.

**Fund F: Fixed-Income Investment Fund**—invested in Barclay's U.S. Debt Index fund, which tracks the Lehman Brothers Aggregate Bond Index. This option aims at matching the performance of the U.S. bond market.

**Fund G: Government Securities Investment Fund**—invested in U.S. Government securities. It is risk-free with a competitive rate of return.

**Fund L: Life-Cycle Fund**—The new life-cycle fund opened to thrift plan investors in August 2005. Think of the L Fund as a "fund of funds." It takes the five funds currently in the thrift plan, and based upon your years to retirement, will do the asset allocation mix for you. Those closer to retirement will have a far more conservative mix than those 15, 20, or 25 years from retirement.

## Rates of return for TSP investment funds*

|  | 2001 | 2002 | 2003 | 2004 | 2005 |
|---|---|---|---|---|---|
| Fund G | 5.39% | 5.00% | 4.11% | 4.30% | 4.49% |
| Fund F | 8.61% | 10.27% | 4.11% | 4.30% | 2.40% |
| Fund C | -11.94% | -22.05% | 28.54% | 10.82% | 4.96% |
| Fund S** | -9.04% | -18.14% | 42.92% | 18.03% | 10.45% |
| Fund I** | -21.94% | -15.98% | 37.94% | 20.00% | 13.63% |
| Fund L | -- | -- | -- | -- | -- |

** Performance for the S and I Fund before 2001 reflect the performance of the Wilshire 4500 (S Fund) and EAFE (I Fund) indexes without deduction of any administrative expenses, trading costs, or investment management fees.

* For current and historical TSP rates check www.tsp.gov/rates

## Inter-Fund Transfers

You can make an inter-fund transfer in any month you wish, without an annual limit. You can transfer or shift any portion of money already in your account to any of the funds available. The most efficient way to request an inter-fund transfer is on-line (tsp.gov) or by using the ThriftLine, 1-877-968-3778.

## Vesting in the TSP

Vesting is acquiring ownership of the agency 1 percent contribution to your Thrift Savings Plan account. Once you are vested, all the money in the account belongs to you and can be taken out of the plan if you leave federal service. All employees are 100 percent vested in their own contributions, the government matching contribution, and the earnings on the account. You are vested in the 1 percent agency contribution after three years of employment.

## Loans from the TSP

A TSP loan program is available. You can borrow what you have contributed and the earnings on those contributions for a variety of reasons. There are two types of loans. You can apply for a general purpose loan with a repayment period of one to five years, or you can apply for a residential loan for the purchase of a primary residence with a repayment period of one to 15 years.

No documentation is required for a general purpose loan, but you must submit documentation to support the amount of a residential loan request. If you are a FERS employee, you can borrow only your portion, not the government's portion. The interest rate is the prevailing rate of interest for the G Fund. In the last few years, with the G Fund interest rates lower, the cost of borrowing from the Thrift Savings Plan has been substantially better than borrowing from banks or credit unions.

With the new record-keeping system came changes to TSP loan policies. New rules allow re-amortization more than once and you may make partial repayments. In addition, loan information will be on your statement, which will be issued quarterly. The TSP charges a one-time application fee for a new loan.

## What are my withdrawal options?

When you retire, you have several TSP withdrawal options:

• You can take your Thrift Savings Plan funds as an annuity. If you select this option, you are taxed only on the amount you receive each month in an annuity.

- Another option is taking your entire Thrift Savings Plan funds in a lump sum. You will pay ordinary income taxes on the entire amount.

- You can choose to receive your account balance in substantially equal monthly payments and pay taxes only on the amounts received.

- New rules allow any combination of the above options for a retiree's full withdrawal. In addition, you may make a one-time partial withdrawal after separation, as long as you did not take an age-based, in-service withdrawal. Withdrawal elections begin after you select a full withdrawal choice.

- If you are eligible for retirement benefits, you can leave the money in the TSP after you leave federal service. You can continue to change investments, but you cannot add to the fund after you retire. You can leave the money in your account until April 1 of the calendar year after you turn 70½. At that time, you will be required to receive a minimal distribution, which will be based on your age and life expectancy.

- You can withdraw your TSP funds at retirement (either voluntary or involuntary). A 10 percent tax penalty for early withdrawal may apply if you separate or retire before the calendar year in which you reach age 55 and withdraw the funds before age 59½. You should refer to the *Summary of the Thrift Savings Plan for Federal Employees* (available upon request from your personnel office) for further information.

- You can elect, at the time you retire, to transfer your TSP funds into another reorganized retirement system. This would be possible if you go to work for some other entity after federal retirement. Your personnel office can check with the TSP Service Office to determine if your new retirement system is a recognized system.

- Another option is to have your agency roll the funds into an IRA. By doing this, you keep these funds tax deferred until as early as age 59½ or as late as age 70½. If there are any questions concerning your withdrawal options, you should check with your personnel office.

# Q&A

**When and how can I withdraw funds from the TSP?** You can withdraw funds from your TSP account while still employed for two reasons: financial hardship, and a one-time single payment (of all or part of your account) for employees over age 59½, without withdrawal penalties.

Hardship withdrawals by employees under age 59½ are subject to early withdrawal penalties. These withdrawals are referred to as "in-service withdrawals" and apply to both CSRS and FERS employees.

**What are the procedures for post-service withdrawals?** All TSP participants who separate from federal service have the same withdrawal options, regardless of their eligibility for retirement benefits. When you separate you become eligible to withdraw your TSP account. You have many options from which to choose, so carefully examine the packet of TSP information you will receive at retirement. Here are some examples:

- You may choose a TSP life annuity, a single payment, or a series of monthly payments.

- You may also leave your account in the TSP when you separate, and make a withdrawal later on.

- You may transfer part or all of your TSP funds to an IRA or other eligible (private industry) retirement plan, but if you choose an IRA or other eligible plan you cannot change your request.

- Also, you may have your payments begin immediately or at a later date,but not beyond your minimum required distribution age of 70½.

These options are sometimes called "mix and match" withdrawals. Under the new regulations, you have a greater choice than was previously available.

**How does the cost of health insurance change when I retire?** The cost of health insurance does not change when you retire. You pay the same as when you were an employee. The federal government pays the same. The basic difference is that you pay the premium on a monthly basis usually out of your annuity check.

**If both my spouse and I are federal employees,** is it necessary for either or both of us to elect a survivor benefit to ensure that the surviving spouse will have health insurance? No, neither of you will be required to elect a survivor benefit as long as you were both covered by federal health insurance at retirement and you submit an SF2809 for verification of your coverage.

**I started at age 22, can I leave at age 52?** It depends; retirement benefits have specific age and service requirements. CSRS requires age 55 with 30 years of service; age 60 with 20 years of service; age 62 with five years of service. Therefore, at age 52 with 30 years of service, you would not meet the eligibility requirement. You would have to wait until you were age 55.

FERS requires age 62 and five years of service; age 60 and 20 years of service; or MRA (minimum retirement age) and 30 years of service. Your MRA is based on the year of your birth. FERS employees can also retire at the MRA and 10 years of service (benefits are reduced by 5 percent for your years under age 62).

So the quick answer is "no" for CSRS and "maybe" for FERS employees if the specific requirements are met.

**Can I count sick leave?** Sick leave counts (for CSRS only) in the computation of your annuity after you have met all the eligibility requirements for an immediate annuity.

**Does locational pay count toward retirement?** Locality pay counts toward your high-3 salary and is used in the formula that determines your retirement pay.

**If my spouse dies before I do, what happens to the cost/survivor benefits?** The reduction for survivor benefits stops and your annuity increases. The money you have paid for the spousal survivorship is not refunded to you.

**Does my ex-spouse have rights?** Ex-spouses have certain rights under the provisions of the Spouse Equity Act. For example, a court may award a survivor annuity and/or TSP benefits to a former spouse.

**If my disabled child receives a Social Security benefit does it affect my benefits?** A disabled child receiving Social Security benefits would not affect benefits you would receive.

**Can I leave a benefit to a child?** Children are provided death benefits if they are under 18 and unmarried. An annually adjusted amount is determined by the number of children. Benefits may continue until age 22, if the child is in school. For FERS employees/annuitants, the child's benefits are reduced by any Social Security benefits the child receives. Benefits to children are provided without cost to the employee/annuitant.

**What am I entitled to if I quit?** If you have retirement eligibility you could draw a pension, you could leave your money in the retirement system and draw a deferred retirement annuity at age 62, or you could withdraw all your retirement funds.

**When should I retire?** You should retire when you are eligible and want to retire. There is no magic formula that makes the decision for you.

**When will my annuity begin and will it be taxed?** If you are CSRS your annuity begins the next day—if you retire the last day of the month or the first, second, or third day of the month you become eligible. If you are FERS, your annuity begins the next day if you are eligible to retire on the last day of the month. Absolutely, your annuity will be taxed from Day One!

**Are there differences between how states tax an annuity?** Every state is different in how it taxes annuities and some do not tax an annuity at all. Alaska, Florida, Nevada, New Hampshire, South Dakota, Tennessee, Texas, Washington, and Wyoming have no personal income taxes. Alabama, Hawaii, Illinois, Kansas, Louisiana, Massachusetts, Michigan, New York, and Pennsylvania exempt the total amount of a civil service annuity from taxation. In Kentucky, North Carolina, Oregon, and Wisconsin varying amounts of an annuity are exempt. Check with your state for specific laws.

**If I postpone retirement, what happens to my health insurance?** Nothing. If you postpone retirement you pay just as you do now. Your health insurance premiums do not change in retirement.

**How might Medicare Plus (state) affect my benefits/my Medicare?** It would not affect your retirement benefits or your entitlement to Medicare.

**How will I know that my application for retirement is being processed?** Upon receipt of your retirement application from your personnel and payroll office, OPM will notify you that your application is being processed. They will provide you with a civil service claim identification number (e.g., CSA0000000). This number is required whenever you, or anyone on your behalf, contacts OPM concerning your annuity.

**Who should I contact if I have questions before I receive a CSA number?** It normally takes about 30-45 days for OPM to issue a CSA number. If you need to check on the status of your application, you should contact your former payroll office to determine when your records were sent to OPM. Your payroll office should provide you with the number and date of the Register of Separations and Transfer. You will also need your payroll identification number.

**Can I receive payments before my claim is processed?** As soon as OPM receives all of your records, they will begin making "interim payments." These interim payments normally begin within one to three months after the date of retirement. Interim payments can only be authorized if your records clearly show that you are eligible for retirement.

**How much will my interim payment be?** Interim payments average approximately 85 percent of your projected final benefit. However, they may be less if:

1. You have received a refund for retirement deductions previously paid;

2. You have service after Oct. 1, 1982, not covered by the retirement system; or

3. You have service for which you have not made a deposit or redeposit. Interim payments are subject to federal withholding tax. No premiums for health or life insurance will be withheld until you are placed in permanent pay status.

**When are my checks due?** Monthly checks are due the first business day of the month.

**When will I be placed in permanent payment status?** The majority of retirees are placed in permanent payment status within the first four months after retirement. At the time you are placed in permanent payment status, you will receive a refund of the amount withheld from your interim payments minus the premiums for health and life insurance.

## CSRS Sick Leave Chart

### Chart for Obtaining Number of Days/Months  When 2,087 Hours Constitutes Yearly Basis

| Days | 1 Day and up | 1 mo. and up | 2 mo. and up | 3 mo. and up | 4 mo. and up | 5 mo. and up | 6 mo. and up | 7 mo. and up | 8 mo. and up | 9 mo. and up | 10 mo. and up | 11 mo. and up |
|---|---|---|---|---|---|---|---|---|---|---|---|---|
| 0 | 0 | 174 | 348 | 522 | 696 | 870 | 1044 | 1217 | 1391 | 1565 | 1739 | 1913 |
| 1 | 6 | 180 | 354 | 528 | 701 | 875 | 1049 | 1223 | 1397 | 1571 | 1745 | 1919 |
| 2 | 12 | 186 | 359 | 533 | 707 | 881 | 1055 | 1229 | 1403 | 1577 | 1751 | 1925 |
| 3 | 17 | 191 | 365 | 539 | 713 | 887 | 1061 | 1235 | 1409 | 1583 | 1757 | 1930 |
| 4 | 23 | 197 | 371 | 545 | 719 | 893 | 1067 | 1241 | 1415 | 1588 | 1762 | 1936 |
| 5 | 29 | 203 | 377 | 551 | 725 | 899 | 1072 | 1246 | 1420 | 1594 | 1768 | 1942 |
| 6 | 35 | 209 | 383 | 557 | 730 | 904 | 1078 | 1252 | 1426 | 1600 | 1774 | 1948 |
| 7 | 41 | 214 | 388 | 562 | 736 | 910 | 1084 | 1258 | 1432 | 1606 | 1780 | 1954 |
| 8 | 46 | 220 | 394 | 568 | 742 | 916 | 1090 | 1264 | 1438 | 1612 | 1786 | 1959 |
| 9 | 52 | 226 | 400 | 574 | 748 | 922 | 1096 | 1270 | 1444 | 1617 | 1791 | 1965 |
| 10 | 58 | 232 | 406 | 580 | 754 | 928 | 1101 | 1275 | 1449 | 1623 | 1797 | 1971 |
| 11 | 64 | 238 | 412 | 586 | 759 | 933 | 1107 | 1281 | 1455 | 1629 | 1803 | 1977 |
| 12 | 70 | 243 | 417 | 591 | 765 | 939 | 1113 | 1287 | 1461 | 1635 | 1809 | 1983 |
| 13 | 75 | 249 | 423 | 597 | 771 | 945 | 1119 | 1293 | 1467 | 1641 | 1815 | 1988 |
| 14 | 81 | 255 | 429 | 603 | 777 | 951 | 1125 | 1299 | 1472 | 1646 | 1820 | 1994 |
| 15 | 87 | 261 | 435 | 609 | 783 | 957 | 1130 | 1304 | 1478 | 1652 | 1826 | 2000 |
| 16 | 93 | 267 | 441 | 615 | 788 | 962 | 1136 | 1310 | 1484 | 1658 | 1832 | 2006 |
| 17 | 99 | 272 | 446 | 620 | 794 | 968 | 1142 | 1316 | 1490 | 1664 | 1838 | 2012 |
| 18 | 104 | 278 | 452 | 626 | 800 | 974 | 1148 | 1322 | 1496 | 1670 | 1844 | 2017 |
| 19 | 110 | 284 | 458 | 632 | 806 | 980 | 1154 | 1328 | 1501 | 1675 | 1849 | 2023 |
| 20 | 116 | 290 | 464 | 638 | 812 | 986 | 1159 | 1333 | 1507 | 1681 | 1855 | 2029 |
| 21 | 122 | 296 | 470 | 643 | 817 | 991 | 1165 | 1339 | 1513 | 1687 | 1861 | 2035 |
| 22 | 128 | 301 | 475 | 649 | 823 | 997 | 1171 | 1345 | 1519 | 1693 | 1867 | 2041 |
| 23 | 133 | 307 | 481 | 655 | 829 | 1003 | 1177 | 1351 | 1525 | 1699 | 1873 | 2046 |
| 24 | 139 | 313 | 487 | 661 | 835 | 1009 | 1183 | 1357 | 1530 | 1704 | 1878 | 2052 |
| 25 | 145 | 319 | 493 | 667 | 841 | 1015 | 1188 | 1362 | 1536 | 1710 | 1884 | 2058 |
| 26 | 151 | 325 | 499 | 672 | 846 | 1020 | 1194 | 1368 | 1542 | 1716 | 1890 | 2064 |
| 27 | 157 | 330 | 504 | 678 | 852 | 1026 | 1200 | 1374 | 1548 | 1722 | 1896 | 2070 |
| 28 | 162 | 336 | 510 | 684 | 858 | 1032 | 1206 | 1380 | 1554 | 1728 | 1901 | 2075 |
| 29 | 168 | 342 | 516 | 690 | 864 | 1038 | 1212 | 1386 | 1559 | 1733 | 1907 | 2081 |

# CHAPTER 9

# Personal Data Organizer

*What records are necessary to keep?*
*Where should this information be kept?*
*Is one copy enough?*

THIS IS YOUR PERSONAL PLANNING PORTFOLIO. It provides you and your planning partner with a quick and easy reference for recording information about your key documents. It is designed to allow you to arrange data on all your records simply and concisely.

Record all information as completely as possible. In the event of an emergency or death, this information can be extremely important. Having everything organized means those who must make decisions will have the information necessary to make decisions.

When you are finished with your personal inventory, place it in a safe location known to at least two other family members or close friends. Don't place the information in a safe deposit box because of limited access to it in a time of need.

Finally, try to update this personal planning inventory with your spouse or planning partner once a year. Your time will be well spent.

## Personal Data

**Name** (Maiden Name) _____

Date and place of birth _____

Location of birth certificate _____

Social Security number _____

**Partner's Name** _____

Date and place of birth _____

Location of birth certificate _____

Social Security number _____

## Location of :

Citizenship papers _____

_____

Marriage certificate _____

Military papers DD-214 _____

_____

Divorce papers _____

State of jurisdiction _____

## Parents

Father's Name _____

Date and place of birth _____

Date and place of death _____

Mother's Name _____

Date and place of birth _____

Date and place of death _____

Father's Name _____

Date and place of birth _____

Date and place of death _____

Mother's Name _____

Date and place of birth _____

Date and place of death _____

## Children

NAME _____ TELEPHONE _____

ADDRESS _____

CITY/STATE/ZIP _____

NAME _____ TELEPHONE _____

ADDRESS _____

CITY/STATE/ZIP _____

NAME _____ TELEPHONE _____

ADDRESS _____

CITY/STATE/ZIP _____

NAME _____ TELEPHONE _____

ADDRESS _____

CITY/STATE/ZIP _____

NAME _____ TELEPHONE _____

ADDRESS _____

CITY/STATE/ZIP _____

## Financial Records: Bank/Credit Union Accounts

☐ Checking ☐ Savings
_____
ACCOUNT NUMBER

_____
INSTITUTION                                    TELEPHONE

_____
ADDRESS

_____


☐ Checking ☐ Savings
_____
ACCOUNT NUMBER

_____
INSTITUTION                                    TELEPHONE

_____
ADDRESS

_____


☐ Checking ☐ Savings
_____
ACCOUNT NUMBER

_____
INSTITUTION                                    TELEPHONE

_____
ADDRESS

_____


☐ Checking ☐ Savings
_____
ACCOUNT NUMBER

_____
INSTITUTION                                    TELEPHONE

_____
ADDRESS

_____

## Equity Funds

| Document | Location | Identifying Number |
|---|---|---|
| | | |
| | | |
| | | |
| | | |

## Bond Funds

| Document | Location | Identifying Number |
|---|---|---|
| | | |
| | | |
| | | |
| | | |

## Individual Stock

| Document | Location | Identifying Number |
|---|---|---|
| | | |
| | | |
| | | |
| | | |

## REITs

| Document | Location | Identifying Number |
|---|---|---|
| | | |
| | | |
| | | |

## Cash & Cash Equivalents

| Document | Location | Identifying Number |
|---|---|---|
|  |  |  |
|  |  |  |
|  |  |  |
|  |  |  |
|  |  |  |
|  |  |  |
|  |  |  |

## Personal Creditors or Debtors

| Name | Amount | Location of Record |
|---|---|---|
|  |  |  |
|  |  |  |
|  |  |  |
|  |  |  |
|  |  |  |
|  |  |  |
|  |  |  |

## Tax Records

Location of personal income tax returns and tax return support information

# Safe Deposit Box

COMPANY

ADDRESS

TELEPHONE                                          BOX NUMBER

LOCATION OF KEY

CONTENTS

# Wills

LOCATION OF WILL

LOCATION OF COPY #2

DATE OF WILL

LAWYER                                             TELEPHONE

EXECUTOR                                           TELEPHONE

# Property Records: Automobiles

TITLE LOCATION #1

BILL OF SALE

TAG RECEIPTS

TITLE LOCATION #2

BILL OF SALE

TAG RECEIPTS

# Property Records: Real Estate

ADDRESS #1

TYPE OF PROPERTY

TITLE REGISTERED TO

TITLE INSURED BY

INSURER ADDRESS

INSURER TELEPHONE

MORTGAGE HOLDER

MORTGAGE HOLDER ADDRESS

MORTGAGE HOLDER TELEPHONE

LOCATION: DEED/MORTGAGE COPY

IS MORTGAGE PAID IN FULL?

LOCATION OF RECEIPTS

LOCATION OF TAX RECEIPTS

ADDRESS #2

TYPE OF PROPERTY

TITLE REGISTERED TO

TITLE INSURED BY

INSURER ADDRESS

INSURER TELEPHONE

MORTGAGE HOLDER

MORTGAGE HOLDER ADDRESS

MORTGAGE HOLDER TELEPHONE

LOCATION: DEED/MORTGAGE COPY

IS MORTGAGE PAID IN FULL?

LOCATION OF RECEIPTS

LOCATION OF TAX RECEIPTS

Miscellaneous Notes:

## Personal Property

Jewelry, fine art, antiques, furniture, boats, coins, family items, etc.

| Item | Location | Insured?/Amount |
|------|----------|-----------------|
|      |          |                 |
|      |          |                 |
|      |          |                 |
|      |          |                 |
|      |          |                 |
|      |          |                 |
|      |          |                 |
|      |          |                 |
|      |          |                 |

## Insurance: Life Insurance

GROUP POLICY NUMBER                                          POLICY AMOUNT

POLICY LOCATION

OTHER POLICIES

## Insurance: Medical Insurance

CARRIER

ADDRESS

POLICY NUMBER                        POLICY AMOUNT                        ID NUMBER

OTHER MEDICAL INSURANCE POLICIES

## Insurance: Property Insurance

COMPANY NAME                                                AGENT

ADDRESS

TELEPHONE

POLICY NUMBER                                                POLICY AMOUNT

POLICY LOCATION

# Insurance: Auto Insurance

COMPANY NAME                                              AGENT

ADDRESS

TELEPHONE                                                 POLICY NUMBER

POLICY LOCATION

OTHER POLICIES

# Employment History

PRESENT EMPLOYER

ADDRESS

TELEPHONE                                                 YEARS

BENEFITS DUE

SPOUSE'S PRESENT EMPLOYER

ADDRESS

TELEPHONE                                                 YEARS

BENEFITS DUE

## IRA, 401k, Roth, Deferred Savings, etc.

| Contributions | Amount | Date | Balance | Location |
|---|---|---|---|---|
|  |  |  |  |  |
|  |  |  |  |  |
|  |  |  |  |  |
|  |  |  |  |  |
|  |  |  |  |  |
|  |  |  |  |  |
|  |  |  |  |  |
|  |  |  |  |  |

## Attorney

NAME                                                                    TELEPHONE

ADDRESS

## Doctor

NAME                                                                    TELEPHONE

ADDRESS

## Accountant

NAME                                                                    TELEPHONE

ADDRESS

## Insurance Agent

NAME                                          TELEPHONE

ADDRESS

## Banker

NAME                                          TELEPHONE

ADDRESS

## Broker

NAME                                          TELEPHONE

ADDRESS

## Executor of Estate

NAME                                          TELEPHONE

ADDRESS

## Clergy

NAME                                          TELEPHONE

ADDRESS

## Other important contacts

_____

_____

_____

_____

_____

_____

_____

_____

_____

_____

_____

## Notes

_____

_____

_____

_____

_____

_____

_____

_____

_____

_____

_____

## Financial Planning/Cash Planning

Belsky, Gary and Thomas Gilovich, *Why Smart People Make Big Money Mistakes*, Fireside, 2000.

Benna, R. Theodore, *Escaping the Coming Retirement Crisis: How to Secure Your Financial Future,* Colorado Springs, CO: Pinon Press, 1995.

Buffett, Mary, *Buffettology*, Rawson Associates, 1997

Evans, Richard E., *The Index Fund Solution*, Simon & Schuster, 1999.

Garner, Robert J., *Ernst & Young's Personal Financial Planning Guide*. New York: J. Wiley & Sons, 1995.

Goodman, Jordan Elliot, *Everyone's Money Book*. Illinois: Dearborn Financial Publications, 1994.

Irnibm, Suzie, *The Courage to be Rich*, Riverhead Books, 1999.

Jenks, James M., *Employee Benefits: Plain and Simple: The Complete Step-by-Step Guide to Your Benefits Plan*. Toronto, New York: Collier Books, 1993.

Malkiel, Burton G., *A Random Walk Down Wall Street*, W.W. Norton & Company, 8th Editions, 2003.

Morris, Kenneth M., *The Wall Street Journal Guide to Planning Your Financial Future*. New York: Lightbulb Press, 1995.

Orman, Suze, *The Road to Wealth*, Riverhead Books, 2001

Patterson, Martha Priddy, *The Working Woman's Guide to retirement Planning: Saving & Investing Now for a Secure Future,* New Jersey: Prentice Hall, 1993.

Shiller, Robert, *Irrational Exuberance*, Princeton University Press, 2000.

Shiller, Robert, *The New Financial Order:Risk in the 21st Century*, Princeton University Press, 2003.

Sloane, Leonard, *The New York Times Personal Finance Handbook*. New York: New York Times Books, 1995.

Tobias, Andrew, *The Only Investment Guide You'll Ever Need*, Harvest Books, 2002

## Financial Planning—Organizations & Websites

401k/403b Advocate. (*timyoukin.com*) Smart, objective advice, tough site to navigate.

Bureau of the Public Debt (*ustreas.gov/treasury/bureaus/pubdebt*). Find information about U.S. savings bonds, Treasury bills and bonds. Learn of upcoming Treasury auctions, or link to the Federal Reserve Board of New York's on-line savings-bond redemption-value calculator.

Certified Financial Planner Board of Standards. (*cfp-board.org*). Useful consumer section.

CNNfn (*cnnfn.com*) CNN Financial. Find investing ideas and analysis.

College XPress (*collegexpress.com*) Planning, admission, application, school profiles.

Dalbar (a financial research firm) and Microsoft (*therightadvisor.com*) Find planners in your area. Enter the size of your portfolio, the type of planning you need, and your preferences in a planner. Advisors have at least five years of experience, a clean record with financial regulators, and a background in the specialty you request.

Financenter (*financenter.com*). Financial calculators cover a wide array of what-if scenarios concerning your home, car, and credit cards.

The Financial Aid Information Page (*finaid.org*). Connect with college financial-aid offices, link to a database of scholarships and lists of student-aid lenders.

Financial Engines. (*financial engines.com*) Browse scenarios, forecasts, etc.Fees.

Financial Planning Association, (*fpanet.org*), 3801 E. Florida Avenue, Suite 708, Denver, CO 80210-2544, 800-322-4237.

Garrett Planning Network, (*garrettplanningnetwork.com*), a group of advisers who charge by the hour.

Health Insurance Association of America, 202-824-1600, Fax: 202-824-0609, (*hiaa.org*)

Insurance News Network Get rules and rates for about twenty states on choosing auto, home, and life insurance. (*insure.com*).

Internal Revenue Service (*irs.ustreas.gov/prod/cover.html*). Find tax information for individuals and businesses. Search tax regulations and download forms and publications.

The International Association for Financial Planning. (*planningpaysoff.com*)

INVESTools (*investools.com*). Reference financial newsletters and publications by typing the name or symbol of the company; references are displayed, along with hypertext links and cost.

Life-Line. Find a glossary of insurance terms and an on-line calculator which figures life and disability insurance needs. (*life-line.org*)

Morningstar.Net (*morningstar.net*) Get updates from this mutual fund rating firm.

MPower Cafe. (*mpower.com*). Investment advice. A *Forbes* Magazine favorite.

Mutual Funds Interactive (*brill.com*). Explore the basics of fund investing with links to fund home pages and other fund-related Web sites.

National Association of Personal Financial Advisors, (*feeonly.org*) 888-333-6659, (*napfa.org*)

National Foundation for Consumer Credit, 8611 Second Avenue, Suite 100, Silver Spring, MD 20910, 301-589-5600, Fax: 301-495-5623, Office locator 800-388-2227, (*nfcc.org*)

NETworth (*networth.galt.com*). Search the top mutual funds by category or time period. Call up one- sentence descriptions of fund goals and short manager bios.

Quicken Retirement. (*quicken.com/retirement*) User friendly tax, investment, insurance and mortgage information.

Quicken Insure Market. Get instant price quotes on life insurance and nearest agents. Auto insurance quotes are also available. (*insuremarket.com*)

WiredScholar (*wiredscholar.com*). Get side by side comparisons of college costs.

## Legal Issues

Daly, Eugene J., *Thy Will Be Done: A Guide to Wills, Estates, and Taxation for Older Persons.* Buffalo, NY: Prometheus Books, 1990.

Milko, George, *Real Estate: The Legal Side to Buying a House, Condo, or Co-op: A Step-By-Step Guide.* New York: Random House, 1990.

Myers, Teresa Schwab, *How to Keep Control of Your Life After Sixty: A Guide for Your Legal, Medical and Financial Well-Being.* Lexington, MA, 1989.

### Legal Issues—Organizations & Websites

Nolo Press Self-Help Law Center. Find self-help articles on taxes, mediation, estate planning, homeowners, landlords/tenants, etc. (*nolo.com*)

Quicken Family Lawyer 7.0 . Find 74 legally binding documents (wills, trusts, contracts, leases) to protect you and your family. Documents are customized by state and are valid in 49 states and D.C. (*parsonstech.com*)

American Bar Association, 750 North Lakeshore Drive, Chicago, IL 60611-4403, 312-988-5000, (*abanet.org*)

## Health & Wellness

Carpen, Jean, *The Food Pharmacy Guide to Good Eating.* New York: Bantam Books, 1991.

Gordon, Michael, *Old Enough to Feel Better: A Medical Guide for Seniors.* Baltimore: Johns Hopkins University Press, 1989.

Hales, Dianne R., *Caring for the Mind: The Comprehensive Guide to Mental Health.* New York: Bantam Books, 1995.

Harrell, Keith, *Attitude is Everything.* New York, Cliff Street Books, 2000.

Leatz, Christine Ann, *Career Success/Personal Stress: How to Stay Healthy in a High-Stress Environment.* New York: McGraw-Hill, 1993.

Powell, Robin, *The Working Woman's Guide to Managing Stress.* New Jersey: Prentice Hall, 1994.

*The Physician's Desk Reference: Family Guide to Nutrition and Health.* Montvale, New Jersey: Medical Economics, 1995.

## Aging Parents/Adult Children

Greenberg, Vivian E., *Children of a Certain Age: Adults and Their Aging Parents.* New York: Lexington Books, 1994.

## Family Issues—Organizations & Websites

National Family Caregivers Association, 800-896-3650, offers support and information. (*nfcacares.org*).

National Association for Home Care, 202-547-7424, offers How to Choose a Home Care Provider: A Consumer Guide, write to 228 7th Street, S.E. Washington, D.C. 20003. (*nahc.org*)

U.S. Administration on Aging offers details on local resources and links to other useful Web sites (*aoa.gov*).

Eldercare Locator, 927 115th Street, N.W., 6th Floor, Washington, DC 20005, 800-677-1116. Identifies state and local agencies on aging that can refer you to local services by zip code area. 800-677-1116. (*aoa.dhhs.gov*)

Visiting Nurse Association of America can identify local visiting nurse agencies that operate in forty states, 888-866-8773, (*vnaa.org*).

American Association of Retired Persons (AARP), (*aarp.org/caregiver*) for details on types of help available, CaregiversCircle (*aarp.org/healthguide*) posts questions and comments.

Elder care Web. Find resources for the elderly and their caregivers. State specific information is included. (*ice.net/~kstevens/ELDERWEB.HTM*)

Elderhostel, 75 Federal Street, Boston, MA 02110-1941, 877-426-8056 (*elderhostel.org*)

Geriatric Care Managers, 1604 N. Country Club Road, Tucson, AZ 85716, 520-881-8008

## Career Planning/Workplace Changes

Battle, Carl W., *Smart Maneuvers: Taking Control of your Career and Personal Success in the Information Age*, New York, Allworth Press, 1994.

Bronte, Lydia, *The Longevity Factor: The New Reality of Long Careers and How It Can Lead to Richer Lives*. New York: Harper Collins, 1993.

Brown, Carolann Doherty, *100 Questions Every Working American Must Ask*. Dearborn Financial Pub., 1996.

Cuozzo, Jane Hershey and S. Diane Graham, *Power Partners: How Two-Career Couples Can Play to Win*, New York, Master Media, 1990.

Dent, Harry S. Jr., Job Shock: *Four New Principles Transforming our Work and Business,* New York, St. Martin's Press, 1995.

Krannich, Ronald L. and Caryl Rae Krannich, *Best Jobs for the 21st Century*, 3rd Edition, Manassas Park, VA, Impact Publications, 1998.

Krannich, Ronald L. and Caryl Rae Krannich, *Recareering in Turbulent Times*, Manassas Park, VA, Impact Publications, 1998.

McDermott, Lynda C., *Caught in the Middle*, Englewood Cliffs, NJ, Prentice Hall, 1992.

Peters, Tom, *The Pursuit of Wow!*, New York, Vintage Books, 1994.

Shingleton, John P., *Mid-Career Changes: Strategies for Success*. California: Career Pub., 1993.

Solomon, Muriel, *Getting Praised, Raised, and Recognized*, Englewood Cliffs, NJ, Prentice Hall, 1993

Yate, Martin, *Beat the Odds: Career Buoyancy Tactics for Today's Turbulent Job Market*, New York, Ballantine Books, 1995.

## Career Planning—Organizations & Websites

BrilliantPeople. (*brilliantpeople.com*). Helps find the right recruiter or customize a job search.

CareerMosaic. Use the Career Resource Center to learn to write a resume; research job trends, industries and companies. Find job listings (including international opportunities) and links to employers' home pages. (*careermosaic.com*)

Futurestep (*futurestep.com*). Highly competitive on-line recruitment site with limited (12,000) listings.

The Monster Board. Search for jobs by location, discipline or company and post an on-line resume. Free access to more than 350 companies with job listings. (*monster.com*)

## Social Security, Pensions, Savings

Donlan, Thomas G., *Don't Count on It!: Why Your Pension May Be in Jeopardy ... and How to Protect Yourself*. New York: Simon & Schuster, 1994.

Ferguson, Karen, *Pensions in Crisis: Why the System is Failing America and How You Can Protect Your Future*. New York: Arcade Pub., 1995.

Landis, Andy, *Social Security: The Inside Story: An Expert Explains Your Rights and Benefits*. Washington: Mount Vernon Press, 1993.

Miller, Alan J., *Standard & Poor's 401k Planning Guide*. New York: McGraw-Hill, 1995.

## Social Security Websites

Social Security On-Line. Request an estimate of future benefits, apply for a new or replacement card, or get information on benefits programs. You can also check COLAs and current earnings limitations. 800-772-1213. (*ssa.gov*)

## Tax Planning—Organizations & Websites

American Institute of Certified Public Accountants, Harborside Financial Center, 201 Plaza 3, Jersey City, NJ 07311-3881, 888-777-7077, (aicpa.org)

NannyTax. Get information on employment taxes, both federal and state, when you hire household help. (nannytax.com)

# Index

**K**
Keogh 26

**L**
living trust 50-51
living will 48, 50-51, 57, 76
lump sum 25, 95, 98, 130, 133, 147

**M**
MRA 127-129, 131, 149
Medicare coverage 93
military service 112-113, 125-126
Municipal Bonds 27
mutual fund 13, 17, 22, 26, 29-36, 38-39, 43

**N**
Networking 106
nursing home 80, 82, 85

**O**
Offset 96, 116, 119-122
Open Seasons 123, 135, 140, 145

**P**
part-time work 105, 113
pension plan 2, 76, 95-99
physicians 59, 66
portfolio 11-13, 31, 35-36, 40-42, 106, 153
power of attorney 47, 49-51, 57
precious metals 30, 37
prenuptial agreements 52-53
pyramid of investment 14

**R**
recession 38-40
redeposit service 114
reduced benefits 92, 127
relocation 85-88
retirement housing 81
reverse annuity mortgage 82
revocable living trust 51
Revocable trust 57
Roth IRA 22, 25

**S**
savings bonds 17, 18, 26
second career 5, 103, 105, 107
series EE bonds 17-18
sick leave 113, 115-116, 126, 149, 152
special annuity supplement 131
stock options 38
stocks 12, 20, 28-29, 31-32, 35-36, 38-39
stress 64, 68-71, 75
summary plan description 96

**T**
target heart rate 66
tenancy in common 53
tenants by the entireties 53
term insurance 15-16
treasuries 18-19
treasury bills 9, 18
treasury bond 19, 26-27, 30
trusts 50-51, 55

**U**
Umbrella policy 16
Universal Life 16

**V**
variable annuities 21
variable universal life 16
vesting 97, 146
voluntary contribution accounts 122

**W**
wage base 90
Whole Life 16
Wills 47-48, 79